The Happiness Blueprint

Navigating Life's Challenges on the Road to Happiness

Ana Pachuashvili

Preface

In our pursuit of a better tomorrow, we invest in education, save for retirement, and make decisions that impact our future. But what happens when our future selves don't turn out as we imagined? We may have planned for a successful career, but find ourselves unfulfilled. Or we may have saved for years to travel, but find ourselves too ill to enjoy it. These situations are similar to a writer who spends months crafting a novel, only to have it rejected by publishers or a chef who creates a new dish that no one likes.

It is important to recognize that our future selves are not simply an extension of our present selves. They have their own personalities, experiences, and needs that may differ from ours. As leaders, we may prepare everything necessary for our successors' success, but they may still reject or modify our previous methods or decisions. The relationship between leaders and successors is multidimensional and requires us to approach it with empathy and understanding, it's the same with our present and future selves.

For example, parents may sacrifice their own desires to provide a better life for their children, but their children may not appreciate or desire the life they have created. Similarly, a business owner may plan for their company's future, but new leadership may take the company in a different direction.

By accepting that our future selves and successors are independent and unique, we can hope to create a future that they will appreciate and cherish. It is crucial to approach this relationship with compassion and insight, rather than resentment and dissatisfaction.

Have you ever wished you could predict your own future and make decisions based on the path that would lead to the most happiness? For centuries, this has been a puzzle that has fascinated thinkers. Now, in this book, you can explore the scientific insights into how well the human brain can imagine and predict its own future. With a rich tapestry of ideas from fields such as psychology, neuroscience, philosophy, and behavioral economics, you will uncover a new understanding of your own mind. Are you ready to embark on a journey of self-discovery and unlock the secrets of your future self? Then this book is the perfect choice for you.

Part I

The Power of Future-Oriented Thinking and Resilience

Chapter I

Future-oriented Thinking

In the field of psychology, there is a widely held belief that humans are the only creatures capable of true future-oriented thought. While some animals, such as squirrels and birds, may engage in behaviors that hint at a capacity for forward-thinking, it is thought that these actions are largely driven by instinct rather than conscious reflection.

some studies have shown that these animals are able to cache food (i.e., hide it for later consumption) in anticipation of future need.

One study published in 2005 in the journal "Nature" found that Western scrub jays were able to plan for future needs by caching food in a specific location when they knew they would be hungry in the future. The researchers concluded that the jays were capable of "mental time travel," or the ability to remember past events and use that information to plan for future needs.

Similarly, a study published in 2010 in the journal "Animal Behavior" found that grey squirrels were able to plan for future needs by hiding nuts in locations where they were likely to be hungry in the future. The researchers suggested that the squirrels were using a cognitive map of their environment to plan for future needs.

However, it is important to note that while these studies provide evidence of some capacity for future-oriented thought in certain animals, the extent and nature of this capacity is still a subject of scientific debate.

Humans, on the other hand, are uniquely able to envision a future that does not yet exist, and to take purposeful steps towards bringing that future into being. This is evidenced in the ambitious pursuits of children who dream of becoming doctors or astronauts, and devote years of their lives to learning and preparation, even though their desired future is far off. Similarly, companies invest millions in research and development, hoping to create products that will shape the future of their industry.

Some prominent examples of future thinking individuals and companies include Elon Musk, Steve Jobs, Amazon, Greta Thunberg, and Toyota.

Elon Musk has garnered widespread recognition for his ability to envision a future that does not yet exist. Through his endeavors such as SpaceX, Tesla, and The Boring Company, he has demonstrated a keen focus on creating a sustainable and multi-planetary future.

Steve Jobs, the late co-founder of Apple, was a pioneer in the tech industry and known for his innovative thinking. He had an uncanny ability to predict what consumers would want in the future, leading to the development of groundbreaking products such as the iPhone and iPad.

Amazon has always been a forward-thinking company, consistently investing in research and development to create new products and services that shape the future of commerce and technology. From its early days as an online bookstore to its current status as a global retail giant.

Greta Thunberg, a young climate activist, has become an influential voice in the fight against climate change. Through her passion for a sustainable future, she has inspired millions of people around the world to take action and push for change.

Finally, Toyota has been a leader in innovation within the automotive industry for decades. With a focus on creating hybrid and electric vehicles that are more environmentally friendly, the company is committed to creating a future with zero emissions.

It is this ability to plan for an unseen future that truly sets human beings apart from other animals. By embracing the importance of forward-thinking, we can create a better world for ourselves and future generations. In this way, our species' defining feature is our unique ability to imagine and shape a future that is yet to come.

In his book "The Man Who Mistook His Wife for a Hat," neurologist Oliver Sacks explores the remarkable abilities of the human brain, including its imaginative capacity to conjure up entire worlds that do not exist. Sacks highlights the case of a patient who, despite being unable to form new memories, was still able to imagine and plan for the future based on his past experiences.

The patient that Oliver Sacks refers to in his book is known as "Jimmy" in order to protect his identity. Jimmy suffered from a severe case of Korsakoff's syndrome, which is caused by a thiamine deficiency and often seen in chronic alcoholics. This condition causes damage to the brain, particularly the region responsible for memory, and results in the inability to form new memories.

Despite this limitation, Jimmy possessed an extraordinary ability to construct elaborate scenarios and plan for the future. He was able to draw on his past experiences and piece them together to create richly detailed and vividly imagined situations, such as a hypothetical trip to the beach or a visit to a museum.

What was most remarkable about Jimmy's imaginative capacity was his ability to seamlessly integrate his imagined scenarios into his daily life. For example, he would wake up in the morning and immediately begin preparing for the day ahead, based on the scenarios he had constructed in his mind. He would shower, shave, and dress himself, all while mentally rehearsing his imagined plans.

Sacks described Jimmy's condition as a "breakdown of memory," but also as a "rebirth of imagination." The loss of his memory had forced Jimmy to rely on his imagination in order to construct a coherent sense of self and a purposeful life.

Jimmy's case offers a fascinating glimpse into the creative potential of the human brain. Despite the profound limitations imposed by his condition, Jimmy was able to tap into his imaginative capacity in order to construct a meaningful and purposeful existence. His story underscores the resilience and adaptability of the human mind, even in the face of profound cognitive challenges.

Psychologist Daniel Kahneman, in his book "Thinking, Fast and Slow," discusses the power of the brain's imagination to shape our perceptions and decision-making. He describes how our brains constantly make predictions and judgments based on incomplete information, using mental shortcuts or "heuristics" that can sometimes lead us astray.

In the realm of psychology, it is well-established that our brains frequently employ heuristics, when making predictions and judgments based on incomplete information. These heuristics can be both helpful and harmful, as they can aid in decision-making, but can also lead us astray.

One common heuristic is confirmation bias, which occurs when our brains seek out information that confirms our existing beliefs or opinions. For example, if we believe that a particular political party is superior to another, we may only read news articles that support that view, while ignoring any that contradict it.

Another heuristic is the availability heuristic, whereby our brains rely on information that is easily accessible or memorable. This can cause us to overestimate the likelihood of rare events that receive extensive media coverage, such as plane crashes, while underestimating the risk of more common events, like driving.

The anchoring bias is yet another heuristic, wherein our brains heavily rely on the first piece of information we receive when making a decision. For instance, in a salary negotiation, the first number mentioned can greatly influence the final agreed-upon amount.

The representativeness heuristic is another mental shortcut, where our brains tend to categorize things based on how well they fit our mental prototypes or stereotypes. This can cause us to make inaccurate judgments or assumptions about people or situations. For example, we may assume that a person wearing a suit and tie is a business executive, even if they are actually a musician or artist.

The framing effect can also influence our perceptions and decision-making. The framing effect refers to how the way information is presented can alter our judgments or decisions. For example, if a product is advertised as "90% fat-free," we may be more likely to buy it than if it is advertised as "10% fat."

These heuristics and biases are just a few examples of how our brains use mental shortcuts to make sense of the world around us. While they can be useful in certain situations, they can also lead to errors and biases that impact our ability to make rational and informed decisions. By understanding these heuristics and biases, we can work to recognize and overcome them, leading to more accurate perceptions and better decision-making.

Similarly, in "The Power of Habit," author Charles Duhigg explains how the brain's ability to make predictions and anticipate future events is key to forming habits and changing behavior. By identifying and modifying the cues and rewards that drive our habits, we can use the brain's imaginative powers to transform our lives.

The book provides various examples that highlight the power of these predictive abilities.

For instance, when developing a habit of exercising regularly, one can identify a cue, such as putting on workout clothes, which triggers the brain to anticipate the rewarding feeling of physical activity. Over time, the brain starts to crave the endorphins and sense of accomplishment that come from exercise, making it easier to stick to the habit.

Similarly, modifying cues and rewards can help develop a habit of eating healthier. For example, replacing the cue of reaching for a bag of chips with grabbing a piece of fruit can help the brain associate the healthy snack with a satisfying reward, such as feeling energized or proud of making a healthy choice.

On the other hand, when breaking a habit like smoking, one can identify and modify the cues and rewards that drive the behavior. Avoiding triggers, such as places or people that make one want to smoke, and replacing the habit with a healthier alternative, such as chewing gum or going for a walk, can help the brain learn to associate the new habit with a rewarding feeling, making it easier to stick to the change.

For those struggling with procrastination, using the brain's predictive powers to create a habit of taking action can be helpful. Identifying a cue, such as setting a timer for 5 minutes of work, can trigger the brain to anticipate the rewarding feeling of progress and accomplishment. Over time, the brain learns to associate the cue with the satisfying feeling of making progress, making it easier to overcome procrastination habits.

Overall, the human brain's ability to imagine and plan for the future is a remarkable feat that has been studied and celebrated by psychologists and neuroscientists alike. From predicting the outcome of a chess match to envisioning a future career path, our brains are consistently involved in the cognitive process of anticipating and predicting what will occur next.

As we go about our daily lives, it's easy to overlook just how much our brains are constantly predicting the future. But a wealth of scientific research has shown that these predictive abilities are truly remarkable. For example, studies have shown that when we walk on different surfaces, such as sand or concrete, our brains automatically adjust the tension in our knees to ensure that we don't stumble or fall. However, sometimes our brains' predictions don't come true, and we're met with surprise. This feeling of surprise can be incredibly powerful, revealing that we were expecting something different, even if we weren't consciously aware of it. This phenomenon has been studied in both monkeys and babies, who have been shown to experience surprise when their expectations are violated.

In a classic experiment by Murray and colleagues, monkeys were trained to associate certain visual stimuli with specific outcomes. For example, a particular image may have signaled the delivery of food. However, during the experiment, unexpected events were introduced, such as delivering a different outcome than expected for a given stimulus. The researchers observed the monkeys' behavioral and neural responses to these surprising events. The study found that unexpected outcomes triggered increased neural activity in areas associated with attention and learning, suggesting that monkeys experience surprise and engage cognitive processes to update their expectations.

In developmental psychology, the "Violation of Expectation" paradigm is commonly used to study surprise in infants. In these experiments, researchers present infants with events that violate their expectations based on their prior knowledge of the physical world. For example, a ball appearing to pass through a solid wall. By measuring infants' gaze patterns, researchers can assess their surprise or interest in the unexpected event. If infants show prolonged looking or increased attention towards the unexpected event, it indicates that they have detected the violation of their expectations and are surprised.

These experiments demonstrate that surprise can be used as a measurable signal of the predictive power of the brain. By analyzing patterns of neural activity, scientists can determine when the brain is making predictions and when those predictions are being contradicted, leading to the experience of surprise.

One example of this phenomenon is when we mistake a stranger for someone we know. As we approach the person, we realize our mistake, and this realization can be accompanied by surprise. Similarly, when we watch a magic show and the magician performs a trick that we can't explain, our brain was expecting one thing based on our understanding of the world, but what we saw was completely unexpected and surprising.

Our brains also rely on past experiences to predict the tastes of food. When we bite into something that we thought was sweet but turns out to be sour, our brain was expecting a different taste based on our past experiences. This sudden shift in taste can be surprising and even jarring.

Waiting for someone who is running late can also lead to moments of surprise. When someone who looks like our friend walks in, we might feel a surge of excitement, only to realize that it's not actually them. This moment of disappointment can be accompanied by surprise.

The phenomenon of surprise when our expectations are violated can occur in a variety of everyday situations, and understanding it can help us better understand the ways in which our brains process and predict the world around us.

Within the realm of human cognition lies a treasure trove of valuable insights. Our brains possess a profound capacity for imagination, enabling us to envision and plan for the future. Alongside this power, we must be aware of the biases that shape our perceptions and decisions. Recognizing and understanding these biases empowers us to make wiser choices. Our minds are adaptable and resilient, finding creative solutions even in the face of cognitive challenges. By embracing our brain's predictive abilities, we can shape our lives, cultivate beneficial habits, and navigate the surprises that accompany our journey.

Chapter II

Navigating Optimism Bias for a Resilient Future

In this chapter, we will explore the fascinating world of optimism bias - the tendency to be more optimistic than realistic when predicting the future. This bias is something that affects us all, and can have a significant impact on our decision-making and emotional experiences.

Let's start with an example. Imagine you are planning a vacation with your family. You have high hopes for a perfect, stress-free getaway, and you can already picture yourselves lounging on the beach and enjoying the sunshine. However, when you arrive at the hotel, you discover that the rooms are smaller than you expected, the beach is crowded, and the weather is unpredictable. Your optimistic expectations quickly turn into disappointment, and your mood is ruined for the rest of the trip.

This is just one example of how optimism bias can lead to unrealistic expectations and ultimately, disappointment. However, it's not all bad news - optimism bias can also have adaptive effects. For instance, it can motivate us to pursue challenging goals and maintain hope in the face of adversity.

So, what causes optimism bias? According to scientific research, optimism bias is rooted in cognitive and neural processes. We tend to pay more attention to positive information, remember it more vividly, and use it to form optimistic beliefs. At the neural level, optimism bias is associated with activation in the prefrontal cortex, amygdala, and striatum, which are involved in reward processing, emotion regulation, and decision-making.

But optimism bias is not a one-size-fits-all phenomenon - it can be influenced by various situational and individual factors. For example, people tend to be less optimistic when they are in a negative mood, when they receive feedback that contradicts their beliefs, or when they have prior experience with failure. Some people are also more prone to optimism bias than others, depending on their personality traits, cognitive style, and cultural background.

So, what can we do to mitigate optimism bias? Cognitive strategies such as seeking out diverse sources of information, considering multiple scenarios and outcomes, and engaging in critical thinking and reflection can help us make more accurate predictions and decisions. Mindfulness and meditation practices have also been found to reduce optimism bias and increase awareness of present-moment experiences.

Optimism bias is a complex and multifaceted phenomenon that has both benefits and costs. By understanding the underlying mechanisms and consequences of our biases, we can develop more realistic and adaptive ways of thinking about the future.

Research has shown that people tend to overestimate the likelihood of positive events happening to them and underestimate the likelihood of negative events happening to them. This phenomenon is known as the optimism bias. For example, people tend to believe that they are less likely to experience negative life events such as divorce, illness, or job loss than others. They also tend to believe that they are more likely to achieve success in their careers or personal lives than others. This bias is evident across different cultures and ages, suggesting that it is a universal human tendency.

One study conducted by Tali Sharot and her colleagues at University College London found that people tend to overestimate their likelihood of experiencing positive events by an average of 20%. The researchers also found that people tend to be more optimistic about events that are personally relevant to them, such as their own health or job prospects. In another study, researchers at the University of California, Los Angeles found that people tend to overestimate their likelihood of success in tasks that are difficult or uncertain.

While our optimism bias can make us feel good in the present, it can also have negative consequences for our future. Unrealistic expectations can lead to disappointment and lower levels of well-being. For example, people who overestimate their likelihood of achieving success in their careers may be more likely to experience job dissatisfaction or burnout when their expectations are not met. On the other hand, people who anticipate negative events are more likely to be resilient in the face of adversity.

Research has also shown that our expectations about the future can have a powerful effect on our behavior. For example, studies have found that people who anticipate positive events are more likely to engage in risky behaviors such as gambling or drug use. This is because they perceive the potential rewards as greater than the potential risks. In contrast, people who anticipate negative events are more likely to engage in cautious behaviors, such as saving money or avoiding risky situations.

Our expectations about the future can significantly impact our behavior, but it's important to note that neither optimism nor pessimism is inherently good or bad. Instead, they are tools that we can use to navigate life's challenges, and their usefulness depends on how we use them.

Ultimately, the key is to strike a balance between optimism and pessimism and use them appropriately depending on the situation. If someone is overly optimistic or pessimistic, they may miss important information or opportunities, and their behavior may not align with their goals or values. Therefore, it's crucial to maintain a healthy perspective and remain open to new information and experiences.

So, how can we prepare ourselves for the future while avoiding the negative consequences of our optimism bias? One approach is to engage in what psychologists call "mental contrasting." This involves visualizing both the positive outcomes we hope to achieve and the potential obstacles that may stand in our way. By considering both the positive and negative aspects of the future, we can create a more realistic and balanced view of what lies ahead.

In today's fast-paced and goal-driven world, many of us strive for success and happiness. We set our sights on personal or societal goals, envisioning a better future for ourselves and others. But, as we move forward, we may encounter obstacles that test our resolve and motivation. These challenges can sometimes leave us feeling frustrated, defeated, and uncertain about our ability to succeed.

Fortunately, there is a powerful psychological tool that can help us navigate these challenges and stay focused on our goals. This tool is called mental contrasting, and it involves four simple but effective steps.

The first step is to identify your positive future, which involves envisioning the desired outcome you hope to achieve. This could be a personal goal, such as getting a promotion or losing weight, or a societal goal, such as making a positive impact on the environment or society. Visualizing this positive future creates a clear and compelling picture of what you want to achieve and motivates you to work towards it.

Next, you must identify the obstacles that stand in your way. These obstacles can be internal, such as fear, self-doubt, or lack of motivation, or external, such as financial constraints or social norms. By acknowledging these obstacles, you can prepare yourself to overcome them and avoid being blindsided by them.

The third step is to contrast your positive future with the obstacles that may stand in your way. By doing this, you can gain a better understanding of the challenges you will face and prepare yourself to overcome them. Imagine what it would be like to confront these obstacles and how you might feel in the face of adversity.

Finally, you must develop an implementation intention or a plan for how you will overcome the obstacles you have identified. This might involve seeking out support from friends or family members, developing new skills, or finding creative solutions to the challenges you face. By doing this, you create a roadmap that can guide you towards your desired outcome.

For example, let's say Jane dreams of starting her own business. She envisions herself as the successful owner of a thriving enterprise that helps other small businesses succeed. However, she also acknowledges the financial risk, lack of experience, and competitive market that may stand in her way. By mentally contrasting these two scenarios, Jane gains a more realistic and balanced understanding of what it will take to achieve her goals. She develops an implementation intention by seeking out the guidance of a business coach, enrolling in entrepreneurship courses, and networking with other successful business owners.

By identifying our positive future, acknowledging the obstacles that stand in our way, contrasting these two scenarios, and developing an implementation intention, we can prepare ourselves for the challenges ahead and stay focused on our goals. With mental contrasting, we can create a more realistic and balanced view of the future and overcome our optimism bias.

Another approach is to engage in "defensive pessimism." This involves imagining worst-case scenarios and planning for them in advance. Research has shown that people who use this strategy are more likely to be prepared for negative events and more resilient in the face of adversity. For example, a study by Julie Norem and Nancy Cantor at the University of Michigan found that people who used defensive pessimism were more successful in academic settings than those who did not.

Do you often find yourself worrying about the worst-case scenario in a situation, and do you feel like your negative thoughts are hindering you from reaching your goals? If you do, you're not alone. However, what if I told you that this negative thinking could actually be transformed into a potent mental tool that can help you succeed? In psychology, defensive pessimism is a mental strategy that involves imagining worst-case scenarios and preparing for them in advance. Although it might seem paradoxical, research has shown that individuals who use this strategy are more likely to be prepared for negative events and more resilient in the face of adversity.

For instance, defensive pessimism can be used in job interviews to improve your performance and be better prepared. Before attending a job interview, envision the worst-case scenario, such as not getting the job or performing poorly during the interview. Plan for these scenarios by researching the company, preparing answers to common interview questions, and practicing your responses. Studies show that individuals who use defensive pessimism in job interviews are more likely to be offered the job than those who don't.

When preparing for an exam, defensive pessimism can motivate you to study harder and seek help from tutors or professors. Imagine the worst-case scenario, such as failing the exam or not obtaining the desired grade. Plan for these scenarios by anticipating difficult questions and studying harder. Research shows that students who use defensive pessimism in academic settings are more successful than those who don't.

Defensive pessimism can also be applied to your health. By envisioning the worst-case scenario, such as developing a chronic illness or being diagnosed with a serious condition, you can plan for these scenarios by maintaining a healthy lifestyle, seeking preventive care, and having a support system in place. This strategy can help you be better prepared and cope better in the face of a health crisis. Research shows that individuals who use defensive pessimism in health-related situations have better outcomes than those who don't.

It's crucial to remember that defensive pessimism should not be used excessively or as a way to constantly dwell on negative thoughts, as this can be detrimental to your mental health. However, when used moderately, defensive pessimism can be a powerful mental tool that helps you prepare for the worst-case scenario and become more resilient in the face of adversity. By applying the strategies discussed in this chapter, you can harness the power of defensive pessimism to achieve success and overcome adversity.

Our tendency towards optimistic thinking about the future can have both positive and negative consequences. While imagining positive outcomes can make us feel good in the present, it can also lead to unrealistic expectations and disappointment in the future. By engaging in mental contrasting and defensive pessimism, we can create a more realistic and balanced view of the future, and prepare ourselves for whatever challenges may lie ahead.

Chapter III

Mindfulness

In this chapter, we embark on a journey of self-discovery and delve into the profound practice of mindfulness. We explore practical techniques and exercises that illuminate the path to inner awareness, enabling us to be fully present in the here and now. So, let us venture forth, integrating the wisdom of both, and unlock the keys to a mindful existence.

The practice of mindfulness offers a wide range of benefits, positively impacting our mental, emotional, and physical well-being. By cultivating present-moment awareness and non-judgmental acceptance, mindfulness reduces stress and anxiety, improves emotional regulation, enhances mental clarity and focus, increases self-awareness, fosters resilience and well-being, improves physical health, and cultivates compassion and empathy. Through mindfulness, we gain the ability to navigate life's challenges with clarity, resilience, and compassion, leading to a more fulfilling and balanced existence.

Begin by harnessing the intensity of direct experience, opening yourself to the vividness of the present moment. Through breath awareness exercises, settle your attention and observe the sensations of the breath entering and leaving your body. Transition into a body scan, gradually moving your attention through each part of your body, noticing any sensations or areas of tension. By engaging your senses, you awaken to the richness of the present moment, cultivating deep awareness of your surroundings and yourself.

Embrace the power of a non-judgmental lens, observing your experiences without biases or evaluations. Through mindfulness meditation, learn to observe your thoughts and emotions as they arise, without attaching judgment or attempting to control them. Expand this practice into everyday mindfulness, where you bring focused attention to routine activities like eating or walking. By cultivating non-judgmental awareness, you free yourself from reactive patterns, fostering self-compassion and acceptance.

Discover the dynamic stillness that lies within action. Engage in walking meditation, where you bring full attention to the sensations of your feet touching the ground and the movement of your body. Extend this practice into your daily activities, such as mindful eating or engaging in conversations. By infusing mindfulness into your actions, you uncover a sense of purpose and authenticity, experiencing the depth of each moment with unwavering presence.

Embrace the ever-present now, free from the burdens of the past and the anxieties of the future. Through breath awareness and body scan exercises, anchor your attention in the present moment, where life unfolds in its entirety. Practice everyday mindfulness, directing your awareness to ordinary activities, and savouring the richness of each experience. By dwelling in the power of now, you awaken to the profound beauty and joy that resides in the present.

Integrate mindfulness into every facet of your life, recognizing that the true essence lies in its seamless presence. Utilize loving-kindness meditation, extending warmth and well-wishing to yourself and others. Engage in daily mindfulness exercises, infusing moments with focused attention and open awareness. By consistently practicing mindfulness techniques and exercises, you cultivate a profound transformation, embodying the art of mindful living and nurturing a deeper connection with yourself and the world.

The combination of practical techniques and exercises empowers us to cultivate inner awareness and embrace the present moment fully. Through awakening our senses, cultivating non-judgmental awareness, finding stillness in motion, embracing the power of now, and integrating mindfulness into every aspect of life, we embark on a transformative journey of self-discovery and profound well-being. Embrace these practices, walk the mindful path, and unlock the boundless potential of a life lived in full awareness.

Chapter IV

Harnessing Prospection for Mastery and Agency

Embedded within the fundamental nature of human psychology is an innate yearning for a sense of mastery over one's surroundings. This potent desire for control, when acted upon, has the potential to exert a profound influence on an individual's psychological and emotional welfare. The brain's propensity to anticipate future events and situations stems from our deep-rooted desire for control, which we seek to exert at every stage of our lives, from infancy to the end of our mortal coil.

Numerous scientific investigations have revealed that the lack of control can have a detrimental impact on an individual's mental and physical health. Studies have shown that older adults who feel powerless over their lives are more prone to experiencing symptoms of depression and anxiety. Similarly, individuals who experience high levels of work-related stress and a lack of control over their work environment exhibit elevated levels of both physical and mental health problems. However, when individuals are granted a greater sense of control over their lives, it can have a beneficial impact on their overall well-being. Recent research indicates that employees who have a greater sense of control over their work experience higher levels of job satisfaction and reduced levels of stress. Additionally, individuals who participate in an intervention designed to enhance their sense of control over their lives experience significant improvements in both their physical and mental health.

It is well established that a sense of control is critical for overall well-being, and this is particularly true in the workplace. Employers who empower their employees by providing them with opportunities to make decisions and take ownership of their work are likely to see increased motivation and job satisfaction. Scientific research has demonstrated that employees who have a sense of control over their work environment are more committed to their organization and experience greater levels of well-being.

For instance, a study conducted on nursing home employees found that employees who were given greater autonomy and control over their work tasks reported higher job satisfaction and lower levels of stress. Similarly, a study conducted on call center employees found that providing employees with greater autonomy over their work schedules led to increased job satisfaction and a reduced likelihood of burnout.

As an employer, providing regular feedback and recognition for employees' work and offering opportunities for professional development and growth can also help employees feel more in control of their career trajectory, which is associated with greater well-being. On the other hand, employees who take ownership of their work by setting goals, actively seeking out learning opportunities, and communicating their needs and preferences are likely to experience greater job satisfaction and a greater sense of control over their work environment. For example, a study on employees in a public health organization found that those who had a higher sense of control over their work tasks and environment had greater job satisfaction and lower levels of stress.

The desire for control is a powerful psychological urge that can lead people to adopt false beliefs about their ability to influence uncontrollable outcomes. These misguided convictions can have detrimental consequences, such as fostering a false sense of security and creating unrealistic expectations. For instance, some individuals may think that they can sway the outcome of a sports game by performing specific rituals or wearing a "lucky" jersey. While these beliefs may bring a temporary sense of comfort and control, they are not rooted in reality and can lead to disillusionment and frustration when the desired outcome fails to materialize.

Like in the story of King Canut where in a display of misguided beliefs and an unwarranted sense of power, King Canute boldly commands the mighty waves to halt and bends the ocean to his will. However, his commands are met with laughter and disbelief from those witnessing the spectacle. The waves, unperturbed by his grandiose gestures, continue their relentless motion, showcasing the indomitable forces of nature. Rising from his throne, King Canute is struck by the realization of his own limitations and the fallacy of his assumptions. In that humbling moment, he grasps the profound lesson of humility, understanding the importance of recognizing and accepting one's boundaries. This experiment serves as a poignant reminder, not only for King Canute but for all who witness it, of the inherent power of nature and the necessity of humility in the face of it.

It is imperative to recognize that there are certain aspects of life that we simply cannot control. Instead of relying on false beliefs, we can attain a sense of comfort and control by concentrating on the things that are within our control, such as our attitudes, behaviors, and responses to situations. Here are some strategies that can help us achieve this goal:

Set realistic goals: Establishing realistic goals that are within our control can help us feel a sense of accomplishment and control. It is vital to recognize that we cannot control everything, and sometimes it is best to focus on what is immediately in front of us.

Cultivate gratitude: By focusing on the things, we are grateful for, we can feel more positive and in control. This practice can also help us shift our perspective away from things that are beyond our control.

Seek support: Surrounding ourselves with supportive individuals can help us feel more in control of our lives. Having people who can offer encouragement, advice, and a listening ear can empower us and make us feel more in control.

In situations where we cannot control the outcome, it is crucial to recognize that disappointment is a natural part of life. Rather than avoiding disappointment altogether, we can focus on developing resilience and coping skills to help us navigate through challenging situations. This may involve building a support network, engaging in self-care practices, and seeking professional help if necessary. Ultimately, finding a balance between striving for control and accepting the limitations of our control is key to achieving a sense of comfort and control in life.

Recognizing the limitations of our control is crucial for maintaining our well-being and adapting to life's challenges. To do so, we need to develop a sense of acceptance and resilience that can help us cope with situations where control is limited.

In the quest to gain more control it is important to avoid the pitfall of micromanaging. Micromanaging is a practice detrimental to productivity and well-being, leaves a lasting impact on both the micromanager and the individuals being micromanaged. When individuals are subjected to excessive control and scrutiny, their creative potential suffers. The lack of trust and autonomy impedes their ability to think freely, stifling innovation and fresh ideas. This lack of engagement dampens the collaborative spirit and hampers the generation of creative solutions.

The toll of micromanagement extends to the micromanager themselves. Burdened with the need to oversee every minute detail, they shoulder an immense responsibility that leads to heightened stress levels and a higher risk of burnout. The perception of inadequate support from team members further compounds the strain. Consequently, the work environment becomes drained of vitality, impacting the overall morale and productivity of the team.

Beyond the individual level, micromanaging disrupts the delicate balance within the team dynamic. The erosion of trust and respect between the micromanager and team members hinders effective collaboration and communication. This breakdown in relationships becomes an obstacle to the team's success, impeding progress and hindering the attainment of shared goals. Furthermore, the micromanager's preoccupation with control blinds them to the potential for growth and development among team members. Missed opportunities for delegation and empowerment limit the team's collective progress and limit their ability to achieve their full potential. The time-consuming nature of micromanagement exacerbates these issues, diverting attention from critical tasks and undermining overall team efficiency.

The detrimental effects of micromanaging extend beyond the surface level. They hinder creativity, strain relationships, contribute to burnout, and impede the success of the team. Understanding the perils of micromanagement is crucial for fostering a healthy and productive work environment, one that values trust, autonomy, and collaborative efforts.

in summary, deep within the human psyche resides an unyielding desire for control, an insatiable quest to shape our destinies and mold the world around us. Yet, as we navigate the intricate tapestry of life, we come face to face with the limitations of our influence. Micromanagement, a product of this unquenchable thirst for control, unleashes unintended consequences, stifling creativity, eroding trust, and impeding collaboration. To navigate these treacherous waters, we must cultivate acceptance and resilience. Mindfulness anchors us in the present, freeing us from the burden of past regrets and future worries, while setting realistic goals empowers us to attain a sense of accomplishment within our grasp. Gratitude shifts our perspective, illuminating the blessings that surround us, and seeking support from trusted allies fortifies our sense of community. By embracing these principles, we shield ourselves from the perils of false beliefs and unattainable expectations, finding solace in the wisdom to accept the irrevocable and the resilience to adapt to the whims of fate. Just as King Canute, in his audacious attempt to command the mighty waves, learned the lesson of humility and accepted the boundaries of his influence, we too must recognize our own limitations and dance harmoniously with the ever-changing currents of life.

Part II

Exploring Inner Happiness

Chapter V

The Perspective from Within

Philosophers have debated the nature of happiness for millennia, while psychologists and neuroscientists have delved into the mechanisms that underlie the experience of happiness. The question of what makes people happy has been the subject of countless studies, but what is happens when someone's life circumstances may contradict the very idea of happiness? Such is the case with conjoined twins, whose lives are often deemed "less worthwhile" by conventional medical wisdom.

Conjoined twins are a rare and fascinating phenomenon that occurs when identical twins fail to separate completely during gestation. The exact prevalence of conjoined twins is unknown, but it is estimated to be about 1 in every 200,000 live births. Depending on the site of the conjoinment, conjoined twins can face a range of physical, emotional, and social challenges. Many conjoined twins require lifelong medical care and may face limitations in mobility, communication, and other areas.

Given the challenges that conjoined twins face, it is perhaps unsurprising that conventional medical wisdom has long held that separation surgery is the best course of action, even if it carries significant risks. The assumption has been that conjoined twins are inherently less happy than other people and that their lives are therefore not worth living. However, recent research challenges this assumption and suggests that conjoined twins can experience happiness and fulfillment in their unique circumstances.

One of the most prominent examples of conjoined twins who have challenged the notion of "less worthwhile" lives is Lori and Reba Schappell, the twins mentioned in the article's introduction. Born in 1961 in Pennsylvania, Lori and Reba are joined at the forehead, with part of their skull and some brain tissue shared between them. Despite their physical limitations, the twins have lived a remarkable life, performing as a country music duo, appearing on numerous television shows, and traveling the world. They have also expressed a deep sense of joy and fulfillment in their unique bond.

The Schappell twins' story has attracted considerable attention from both the media and the medical community. In 2003, the twins were featured in an episode of the TLC documentary series "Joined For Life," which followed their daily lives and explored their feelings about their situation. The twins spoke candidly about their struggles and their determination to make the most of their lives.

The Schappell twins' story raises important questions about what constitutes a "good life" and whether conjoined twins can experience happiness and fulfillment. While there is still much we do not know about the subjective experiences of conjoined twins, recent research suggests that they may be capable of experiencing a wide range of emotions, including happiness.

In one study published in the journal Social Science & Medicine, researchers interviewed 11 pairs of adult conjoined twins to explore their experiences of health, illness, and well-being. The researchers found that the twins' experiences of happiness and fulfillment were shaped by a complex interplay of factors, including their physical health, social support, and sense of autonomy. While some twins reported feeling limited by their conjoinment, others reported feeling a deep sense of connection and meaning in their shared lives.

Another study published in the journal Quality of Life Research examined the experiences of parents of conjoined twins who had decided against separation surgery. The study found that these parents reported high levels of satisfaction with their decision and that they viewed their children's lives as "worthwhile" and fulfilling. The parents also reported that their children displayed a range of positive emotions, including happiness, love, and playfulness.

However, the fact that the twins in question themselves express contentment and a desire to remain together raises deeper philosophical questions about the nature of happiness and what it means to lead a fulfilling life. The conventional medical wisdom may hold that conjoined twins should be separated at birth, but perhaps we should question this assumption and consider the possibility that their lives may not be as miserable as we assume.

In fact, there have been numerous scientific studies that challenge the assumption that conjoined twins are inherently unhappy. For example, a study conducted by the University of California, Los Angeles (UCLA) found that conjoined twins tend to have higher levels of empathy and communication skills than the general population. This is likely due to the fact that they are forced to constantly communicate and cooperate with each other in order to navigate their shared physical space.

Another study conducted by the University of Maryland Medical Center found that the vast majority of conjoined twins who were surveyed reported feeling happy and satisfied with their lives. While the study acknowledged that conjoined twins may face unique challenges and limitations, it also found that many of them are able to adapt and find joy in their lives despite these obstacles.

These studies suggest that the assumption that conjoined twins are inherently miserable may be unfounded. While they may face challenges that are different from those experienced by non-conjoined individuals, this does not necessarily mean that their lives are less fulfilling. Indeed, some conjoined twins may even feel a sense of closeness and intimacy that is difficult to achieve in non-conjoined relationships.

Of course, it is important to acknowledge that not all conjoined twins will share the same experiences or feelings about their situation. Some may feel trapped and unhappy, and it is important to provide them with the support and resources they need to address these feelings. However, it is equally important to recognize that there is no one-size-fits-all approach to the issue of conjoined twins, and that each case should be evaluated on an individual basis.

Moreover, the philosophical and scientific debates surrounding the happiness of conjoined twins raise broader questions about what it means to lead a fulfilling life. While many of us may assume that certain conditions or circumstances are inherently miserable, these assumptions may be based on our own preconceptions and biases rather than objective facts. The case of conjoined twins challenges us to reconsider our assumptions and recognize the complexity and diversity of human experience.

By questioning our assumptions and remaining open to different perspectives, we can gain a deeper appreciation for the diversity and complexity of human experience, and perhaps even learn something new about what it means to lead a truly fulfilling life.

Picture this - you're suddenly jobless. Quite a blow, isn't it? Feels like the floor's just disappeared beneath you. But hold on - rather than plummeting into the depths of gloom, why not view it as a springboard to fresh opportunities? You're now at the threshold of discovering diverse career avenues, honing new skills, or even launching your own enterprise. The strategy is to remain buoyant, embrace change, and seize the initiative.

Let's look at another situation. You're in a job that comes with a hefty salary and status. But, it somehow leaves you drained and dissatisfied. Here's what you need to do - a little introspection. Is it the chunky paycheck and acclaim that light up your life or the simple joys like hobbies, quality family time, and self-care? You might find greater joy in a job with lesser stress or a role that resonates more with your interests and beliefs.

Now, imagine this. You've got a workmate who you feel is being troublesome. But have you ever tried to see the world through their eyes? They might be wrestling with stress or personal dilemmas. The solution here is to empathize and strike up a conversation. You might not be able to fix everything with a snap of your fingers, but it could definitely pave the way for better relations.

Here's a typical one. You've always fancied picking up a specific hobby or skill, but you believe you're "not the right fit" or "past your prime". It's high time you questioned that mindset! You'll be astounded at what you can achieve once you apply yourself to it. Begin with baby steps, practice patience, and you may soon discover you've got more potential than you thought.

In the present digital age, we often find ourselves more glued to screens than interacting with people. This can spawn feelings of seclusion and loneliness. The remedy? Cultivate genuine relationships. It could be as uncomplicated as enjoying a coffee chat with a friend, dialing up a relative, or participating in a community gathering. Keep in mind, human connections are the cornerstone of our wellbeing and they infuse our lives with immeasurable value.

In conclusion, the dynamics of life often present us with challenges that can seem daunting. However, by adopting an optimistic and proactive mindset, we can transform adversity into opportunity. The key to happiness lies not necessarily in external factors such as wealth and prestige, but often in simpler pleasures and aligning with our core values. Empathy and communication can significantly improve our relationships, and challenging our preconceived notions can lead to personal growth. Moreover, despite the digital age's distractions, the importance of fostering real-life human connections cannot be overstated. Remember, each curveball life throws is not a stumbling block but a stepping stone to a richer, more fulfilling life.

Chapter VI

Sensation of Joy

Well, here we go, diving into the intoxicating mystery of happiness, a rather tricky concept to elucidate, don't you think? Just picture yourself trying to describe the emotions stirred by the sight of a smiling grandchild, the exhilarating rush of a job promotion, or even the inviting temptation of a chocolate bar. And let's not sidestep the elation often linked with substances like marijuana. You see, these diverse events spark a similar neural rhythm, a sort of harmonious orchestra in our heads, leading us to classify them under the grand notion of happiness.

It's a real brain-teaser for philosophers, who often argue that our feelings, our subjective experiences, are indescribable. In other words, there's no swapping them out — they're singular, bespoke sensations. Hence, emotional happiness is quite the elusive beast, being inherently subjective and devoid of a solid reference point.

Enter the scientists, the brave pioneers of the brain, who've unleashed their arsenal of high-tech gadgets — such as functional magnetic resonance imaging (fMRI) and electroencephalography (EEG) — in a bid to chart the enigmatic terrain of joy. So, what's their discovery? It appears that happiness has set up camp in specific neural routes, taking residence in regions like the prefrontal cortex, amygdala, and striatum.

Check out this intriguing study where fMRI was used to peer into our brains during social encounters. It found that when we are on the receiving end of praise or support, our ventral striatum, the brain's reward center, illuminates like a festive light show. It's as if our brains are imploring, "Bring on more of this, will you!"

Another team of researchers took a different tack, utilizing EEG to decipher the timing of emotional experiences, including happiness. They stumbled upon the fact that the brain's alpha and beta oscillations in the frontal and parietal regions ebb and flow in sync with the highs and lows of our emotional roller coaster.

But let's not jump the gun. While these studies have indeed revealed some neural correlates of happiness, they fall short of encapsulating the subjective experience of joy. Remember the philosophers' assertion about the non-reducible nature of emotions? Nevertheless, these studies act as signposts, directing us towards a better understanding of the neural underpinnings of emotional happiness.

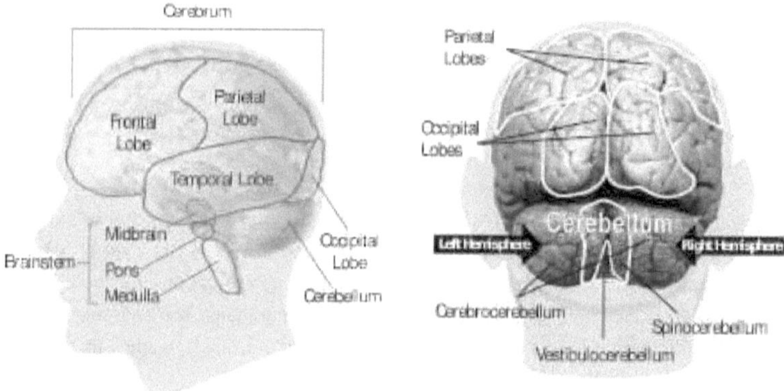

Now, let's shift the focus to genetics. Intriguingly, our genes have a stake in our happiness index, with some fortunate folks genetically wired for higher levels of cheerfulness. But it's not all about the genes; environmental factors also play a pivotal role in the happiness equation.

Aspects like chronic stress, trauma, poverty, and socio-economic disadvantages can be party poopers, making it challenging for individuals to experience happiness consistently. But on the upside, the right kind of environmental influences – like exposure to nature, social support, and meaningful activities – can act as joy amplifiers.

Let's not disregard personality traits. Those besieged by neuroticism, which is linked with heightened negative emotions, might find happiness hard to come by. Conversely, extroverts, generally more susceptible to positive emotions, might find joy more accessible.

And we can't overlook cultural differences. While individualistic cultures like the US value personal happiness, collectivist societies like Japan regard happiness as a shared sentiment, deeply intertwined with social connections and community well-being.

Deciphering happiness is no cakewalk. It's a complex emotion, shaped by a myriad of factors – genetics, mental health conditions, personality traits, life circumstances, and cultural distinctions. But understanding these elements can pave the way towards cultivating more joy and satisfaction in our lives.

In life's unpredictable voyage, we often find ourselves buffeted by the storms of adversity, whether it be trauma, incessant stress, or socio-economic hardships. Amid these tempests, how do certain individuals manage to sustain or even rediscover their happiness? Let's delve into the remarkable resilience of the human spirit and derive inspiration from some truly uplifting real-life narratives. Along this journey, I'll toss in some handy tips that might help you chart your course to happiness amidst the choppy waters of life.

Consider the tale of John, a war veteran who weathered immense physical and emotional distress on the battlefield. After returning home, John found comfort in artistic pursuits like painting and writing, eventually rediscovering a renewed sense of purpose and joy. By transmuting his experiences into art, John exhibited the incredible power of creativity to mend and uplift our spirits, even in the face of tremendous suffering.

When it comes to socio-economic hardships, let's turn to Michael's story. Raised in a low-income neighbourhood, he grappled with numerous obstacles, including limited access to resources and educational opportunities. Undeterred, Michael chased his passion for music with unyielding resolve, eventually blossoming into a successful and fulfilled musician. His narrative underscores the importance of perseverance, passion, and unwavering self-belief.

From these extraordinary tales, we can glean some practical advice on how to sustain or reclaim happiness in the face of adversity:

Use your experiences, both joyful and challenging, as fuel for creative pursuits such as painting, writing, or playing a musical instrument. These activities can offer a therapeutic escape and a fresh perspective on your struggles.

Develop a regular mindfulness meditation practice to stay grounded and focused on the present moment. This practice can enhance your ability to cope with stress and cultivate inner tranquillity, even amidst tumultuous times.

Dedicate time and energy to activities that truly ignite your passion. Engaging in activities that bring joy and purpose can be instrumental in overcoming adversity.

Cultivate strong bonds with friends, family, or support groups who can offer encouragement, understanding, and guidance during challenging times. Having a robust support network can be an invaluable source of strength and happiness.

Celebrate small victories: Break down lofty goals into smaller, manageable tasks, and revel in each accomplishment. Acknowledging your progress, no matter how minor, can bolster your self-confidence and motivation.

Adversity is an inherent part of the human journey. But by tapping into our inner resilience and learning from the inspiring narratives of others, we can realize that happiness is not just possible, but attainable, even amidst the darkest times.

In the whirlwind of our daily existence, nurturing happiness can appear to be a mammoth task. However, with simple strategies and incremental changes, we can indeed construct a happier life. Let's delve into some practical, evidence-based techniques from positive psychology, mindfulness, and cognitive-behavioural therapy, along with some lifestyle adjustments that can steer us towards a more joy-filled existence.

Take a few moments each day to reflect on the things you're grateful for. It could be as simple as enjoying a delightful cup of coffee, basking in the warmth of a sunny day, or cherishing the support of a good friend. By redirecting our focus from the negatives to the positives, we cultivate a more optimistic outlook on life. Consider making it a daily practice to jot down the things you're thankful for. This simple exercise helps shift your attention away from life's challenges and towards its blessings, fostering a greater sense of happiness and well-being.

Incorporate mindfulness into your daily routine by tuning into your present moment experiences, thoughts, and feelings without judgement. This can be achieved through formal meditation, mindful eating, or just focusing on your breath for a few moments. This practice helps to alleviate stress and enhances feelings of well-being.

Learn to spot and challenge negative thought patterns. Techniques from Cognitive-Behavioural Therapy (CBT), like cognitive re framing, can assist you in substituting these pessimistic thoughts with more positive or neutral ones, thereby boosting your mood and reducing anxiety.

Consciously endeavour to savour positive experiences, no matter how trivial. Savouring these moments amplifies the joy they bring and prolongs their influence on your happiness.

Regular physical activity has a proven track record of reducing stress, uplifting mood, and enhancing overall mental health. Find an activity that sparks joy, be it yoga, dancing, hiking, or a leisurely stroll in the park, and make it a routine part of your day.

Relationships are a key component of happiness. Invest quality time with loved ones, nurture supportive friendships, and consider participating in clubs or groups where you can connect with people of similar interests.

Pursue Meaningful Activities: Participate in activities that align with your values and passions. These could be hobbies, volunteering, or even career-related pursuits. Engaging in tasks that hold personal significance can provide a sense of purpose and enhance our life satisfaction.

Ensure you're getting ample sleep, eating a balanced diet, and carving out time to relax and rejuvenate. It's challenging to feel happy if you're physically drained or mentally spent.

Acts of kindness, whether grand or small, can uplift your mood and foster a sense of connectedness with others. This could be as straightforward as holding a door open for someone, volunteering in your community, or simply offering a heartfelt compliment.

Remember, happiness isn't a destination, but a journey. It involves making small, consistent choices that nurture our well-being and promote positivity. While life will always have its peaks and troughs, by incorporating these strategies, we can equip ourselves to navigate the rough waters and cultivate a life abundant with happiness.

Chapter VII

Decoding the Happiness Enigma

Historically, sages have dissected the significance of joy and its link to leading a virtuous existence. Some contend that authentic happiness is a byproduct of moral and meaningful actions, while others appreciate that happiness is a state of feeling, detached from its triggers.

Martin Seligman, a happiness scholar and a psychology heavyweight, has been instrumental in positive psychology, a field he championed. Seligman's endeavors have been geared towards comprehending the happiness and well-being constituents, culminating in his development of the PERMA model. This framework identifies five indispensable elements of well-being: Positive emotion, Engagement, Relationships, Meaning, and Accomplishment.

The PERMA model resonates with the perspectives of ancient philosophers such as Aristotle, who propounded that happiness is not just a transient feeling, but rather the fruit of leading a life with virtue and purpose. According to him, genuine happiness – or eudaimonia – is reaped through the cultivation of virtues like bravery, wisdom, and self-discipline, allowing us to realize our human potential.

Modern scientific investigations reinforce the notion that virtues significantly shape our happiness. Sonja Lyubomirsky, a psychologist, discovered that performing kind deeds could substantially elevate happiness. In her experiment, participants who executed five kind actions per week for six weeks reported enhanced happiness levels than those who refrained. This observation suggests that our decisions and actions, especially those embodying kindness and empathy, can profoundly affect our well-being.

Nevertheless, it's critical to appreciate that happiness doesn't solely hinge on our deeds and virtues. Genetic aspects also considerably sway our happiness levels. Twin studies have revealed that roughly 50% of our happiness is genetically inherited, while a meager 10% is influenced by our life situations. The remaining 40% is steered by our intentional activities – our daily life choices and actions.

The argument that happiness is a feeling state independent of its causes finds backing in the hedonic adaptation research. This principle, also known as the hedonic treadmill, suggests that we swiftly acclimate to life changes – both positive and negative – and revert to a stable happiness level. For instance, people's happiness levels eventually settle to their baseline after striking a lottery jackpot or suffering a significant loss.

The classic research by Brickman, Coates, and Janoff-Bulman (1978) typifies hedonic adaptation. They compared the happiness levels of lottery victors and individuals who had endured a severe accident leading to paralysis. Astonishingly, they found no notable happiness difference between the lottery winners and the accident victims. This observation implies that our happiness levels remain relatively constant even when our circumstances drastically change.

Despite genetics and hedonic adaptation's influence, research has proven that we can actively augment our happiness through intentional activities. Positive psychology interventions, such as practicing gratitude, savoring positive experiences, and engaging in mindfulness meditation, have demonstrated improvements in well-being and happiness.

Likewise, mindfulness meditation research has shown its significant impact on well-being and happiness.

A meta-analysis by Kuyken et al. (2010) found that mindfulness-based interventions, such as mindfulness-based stress reduction (MBSR) and mindfulness-based cognitive therapy (MBCT), could improve mental health, including decreasing symptoms of depression, anxiety, and stress. These findings suggest that cultivating mindfulness, or present-moment awareness, can enhance happiness and well-being.

As we dissect the complex relationship between happiness, virtue, and human nature, it's evident that our well-being is shaped by an array of factors. True happiness seems to entail not only the cultivation of virtues such as kindness, compassion, and mindfulness, but also the acknowledgment of genetics and adaptation's role in our emotional lives.

The central message from this exploration is that while our control over our happiness may be limited, we can significantly sway it through our intentional activities and personal development. By grasping the intricacies of happiness, virtue, and the human experience, we can make knowledgeable choices that foster well-being and empower us to thrive as individuals.

The pursuit of happiness is a nuanced endeavor that demands a detailed understanding of human nature, virtues, and the factors influencing our well-being. By employing the wisdom of philosophers, scientific research, and our personal experiences, we can start to decode the complexities of happiness and strive towards a life of fulfillment and significance.

Part III

Insights into Human Complexity

Chapter VIII

The Complexities of Happiness in the Age of Social Media

This chameleon-like trait of happiness causes a fair bit of head-scratching when it comes to identifying if someone is truly dancing to its tunes.

Not so long ago, a band of intrepid researchers from the University of California decided to decode the enigma of 'happy.' They found that this five-letter word often doubles as a megaphone for individuals to broadcast their life's outlook or stamp their approval, even when joy isn't their current companion. A similar pattern emerged from a study at the University of Missouri, where 'happy' was found to be a flag waved to signal belief in the worthiness of things, emotions notwithstanding.

This insight adds another layer to the happiness maze that scientists are eager to navigate. It appears 'happy' may be a trojan horse, carrying beliefs instead of emotions. But researchers are nothing if not persistent, and they've found a potential compass in human behaviour. True happiness, it seems, leaves footprints in the form of sociability, optimism, and better physical health, among others.

However, the arrival of social media has thrown a proverbial wrench in the works. The relentless parade of 'happy' snapshots online has left individuals grappling with judging its influence on their personal happiness barometer.

A study at the University of Michigan painted a rather melancholic picture of our emotional health in the era of social media. The longer individuals lingered in the virtual world, the more likely they were to feel a gnawing sense of loneliness and depression. The constant yardstick of others' lives often left them feeling like they fell short. A study in the journal 'Cyberpsychology, Behaviour, and Social Networking' nodded in agreement, associating prolonged Facebook use with a dip in life satisfaction and self-esteem. The more individuals leaned on Facebook to measure up, the more their mood took a hit.

But fear not, for there's a silver lining. The gloomy cloud of social media's impact on happiness can be lifted. A combination of limiting virtual interactions and cultivating real-life social connections can do the trick. Several studies have found a direct route to happiness and life satisfaction through face-to-face social interactions. Couple that with a dose of mindfulness, self-compassion, and a focus on individual needs rather than others' lives, and you've got yourself an antidote to the potential emotional pitfalls of social media.

Yet, the relentless pressure to paint a picture-perfect life online can breed insecurity and anxiety, throwing a spanner in the mental health machinery. This phenomenon, known as FOMO (Fear Of Missing Out), seems to have found a cosy home among young adults frequently surfing the social media waves.

FOMO is the gnawing worry of being left on the shore while others sail away on exciting adventures. It's a game of comparison, where individuals weigh their lives against the seemingly flawless ones presented by others on social media. This can crank up the dial on stress and anxiety, and create a feeling of being an island in the sea of connectedness.

Several studies have shown a light on the dark corners of FOMO, revealing a decrease in well-being and life satisfaction and an increase in anxiety and stress levels. What's more, FOMO can create a thirst for validation and social approval that's never quenched.

Fighting off the FOMO beast involves practising mindfulness and zooming in on the positives in one's life, instead of obsessively sizing oneself up against others. This includes limiting time spent on social media, being selective about the content consumed, and fostering meaningful offline relationships and activities.

Social media platforms are designed to keep users hooked, employing tactics that are eerily reminiscent of gambling. The more a user is engrossed, the more the platform scores. One such tactic is the 'variable rewards' system, where the unpredictability of what's next keeps users coming back for more, fuelled by dopamine, the brain's pleasure messenger.

Additionally, these platforms employ 'push notifications' to reel users back in. Each alert is a shot of dopamine, a fleeting satisfaction that soon leaves users wanting more. Social validation, too, is a tool in the platform's arsenal. Each like, share, or comment is a nod of approval that triggers a dopamine release, making us feel good.

Finally, FOMO, too, plays a key role. Social media platforms offer a peek into others' lives, creating a fear of missing out on the highlights. This fear can lead to compulsive checking of the platforms, each check a potential dopamine hit but also reinforcing addictive behaviour.

These tactics combine to make social media platforms as addictive as they are, manipulating our brain's reward system to keep us scrolling, liking, and sharing. It's crucial to understand these mechanisms to use these platforms in a balanced and healthy way. By understanding the dopamine-driven reward system that these platforms use, we can better manage our usage and buffer their potential negative impacts on our mental health.

Chapter IX

Unveiling the Depths of Emotional Connectivity

For centuries, philosophers and thinkers have grappled with the profound question of whether two individuals can genuinely experience the same emotion. Our human experiences are marvelously intricate and inherently personal, defying objective measurement despite our shared language of emotions. Nevertheless, recent scientific inquiries have shed light on this complex quandary, unearthing fascinating insights that challenge our preconceptions. Delving into the realms of color perception, universal emotional aspects, and the subjective nature of our encounters, we embark on a journey to unravel the limits of shared experience.

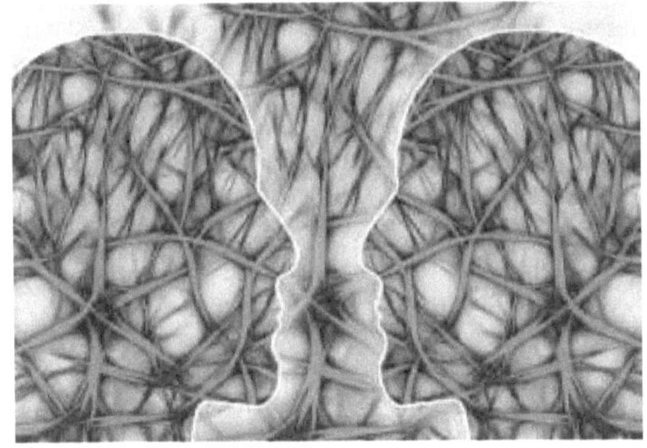

In the realm of color perception, conventional wisdom once asserted that individuals from diverse cultures perceive colors through contrasting lenses. However, contemporary research has debunked this notion, revealing a surprising commonality in our comprehension of basic color categories such as red, blue, and green. This revelation hints at a universal underpinning to our perception of colors, one that is potentially entwined with our biological makeup and evolutionary history. Across cultural boundaries, the threads that connect our understanding of hues weave a tapestry of shared experience, bridging the gap between diverse societies.

Building upon this notion, investigations into cross-cultural emotional responses have illuminated intriguing facets of our shared humanity. Despite the inherently subjective nature of emotions, studies have unearthed remarkable similarities in the way individuals from various cultures experience certain emotions triggered by specific events. A profound loss, for instance, often evokes a profound sense of sadness across cultures, while the presence of imminent danger commonly elicits a surge of fear. These universal threads, interwoven within our emotional fabric, exemplify the interconnectedness that transcends our cultural boundaries.

However, the enigma persists, for the subjective essence of our experiences remains a formidable barrier to ascertaining whether two individuals can genuinely encounter the same emotion. While both may respond to a loss with sadness, the intricate tapestry of their subjective experiences may differ profoundly. It is within these intricacies that our unique personalities, histories, and contextual backdrops shape the lens through which we perceive and interpret our emotions. Thus, shared experience becomes a wistful dance of harmonious chords intermingled with the discordant notes of individual perspectives.

These boundaries of shared experience extend beyond the realm of emotions, permeating a multitude of subjective encounters, such as the perception of taste. Though we may collectively agree that a particular food is sweet, the nuances of sweetness can diverge significantly depending on an individual's genetic makeup, cultural upbringing, and even personal preferences. Similarly, pain, as an intensely subjective experience, manifests uniquely within each individual, rendering its perception an impenetrable fortress of subjectivity.

The limits of shared experience are also pronounced in the domain of sensory perception, particularly in the realm of color. While a collective consensus may emerge that an object is indeed red, the actual experience of the color red can vary dramatically among individuals. Factors such as age, gender, and cultural background cast intricate hues upon the canvas of our perception, rendering our encounter with colors a deeply personal affair.

Akin to sensory perception, aesthetic responses to art form yet another frontier of individualized encounters. While a collective voice may proclaim the beauty and inspiration encapsulated within a particular artwork, the intimate experience of that creation can differ vastly from one individual to another. Personal tastes, cultural backgrounds, and the intricacies of one's perception converge to mold a kaleidoscope of interpretations, painting a rich tapestry of individual responses.

These examples illuminate the kaleidoscopic nature of our experiences and underscore the inherent limits of shared encounter. Our unique histories, personalities, and contextual nuances collectively shape our understanding and interpretation of the world. Consequently, while commonalities exist within our experiences, our subjective encounters diverge significantly. Yet, amidst this realization

lies a glimmer of hope—a recognition of the universal aspects that unite us in our emotional journey and perception of colors.

In the realm of shared experience, the works of philosopher William James resonate profoundly. James aptly observed, "We do not laugh because we are happy; we are happy because we laugh." This simple statement encapsulates the transformative power of empathy—the ability to connect with others, irrespective of the subjective shades that color our individual experiences. By recognizing the universal aspects that bind us, we open doors to genuine understanding, compassion, and the forging of connections across cultural and social divides.

Through the exploration of the boundaries of shared experience, we gain valuable insights into the pursuit of happiness. Despite the intricacies of our subjective encounters, there are universal aspects that connect us as humans. Studies reveal that certain emotions, such as sadness and fear, can be universally triggered across cultures. While the nuances of our experiences differ, empathy allows us to bridge the gap and foster understanding. By recognizing the common threads that unite us, we can cultivate compassion, forge connections, and transcend the limitations of our individuality. In our quest for shared experience, we embrace the complexities that define us, creating a tapestry of empathy that unifies us as one human family and contributes to our collective happiness.

Chapter X

Scientific Insights into the Complexities of Human Experience

A study delving into the influence of experiences on happiness was carried out by researchers from the University of Colorado Boulder and the University of Pennsylvania. The scholars examined how allocating money to experiences, such as traveling or attending concerts, rather than material possessions, impacted happiness levels. The study concluded that experiences offer superior satisfaction and happiness in the long run due to their social and memorable essence.

Imagine a hypothetical situation where a person who had never traveled before suddenly embarks on an extraordinary journey. Upon returning, they profess to be happier as a result. Is their newfound happiness authentic, or has their recent experience shaped their outlook? To comprehend this better, let's consider a study on hedonic adaptation – the human tendency to return to a relatively stable happiness level despite positive or negative life events. Researchers from Northwestern University and the University of California, Riverside discovered that people tend to overestimate the duration and intensity of their emotional reactions to life events. This finding suggests that the happiness derived from novel experiences like traveling may be ephemeral, as individuals eventually adapt to their new circumstances.

However, another study from San Francisco State University indicates that experiences can have a more enduring impact on happiness than material possessions. The researchers found that experiential purchases lead to enhanced well-being and satisfaction compared to material purchases because they contribute to one's sense of identity and social connectedness. This implies that the happiness derived from a life-changing journey may indeed be genuine and long-lasting.

But what about the compelling idea that our present judgments about our past may be erroneous? Research in cognitive psychology has shown that our memories are not as dependable as we might think. Elizabeth Loftus, a renowned memory researcher, has conducted numerous studies demonstrating that memory is pliable and can be influenced by suggestions, misinformation, and even our own emotions. In the context of happiness, this suggests that our recollections of past experiences may not accurately mirror our true emotions at the time.

One study that underscores memory's fallibility is the "reminiscence bump" phenomenon. Researchers have discovered that people tend to recall more positive memories from their adolescence and early adulthood than from other periods in their lives. This can lead to a skewed perception of the past, with individuals believing they were happier during these earlier years than they actually were. The reminiscence bump also illustrates how our experiences act as a filter through which we view life, molding and distorting our memories.

As you immerse yourself in this intellectually invigorating narrative, ponder the role of scientific research in comprehending happiness. In one study, researchers from the University of Utah and the University of Virginia found that people who spent more time in nature reported enhanced psychological well-being and a stronger connection to their environment. This suggests that exposure to natural environments can positively impact happiness, offering another avenue for investigating the intricacies of human experience.

Another influential research domain in the happiness realm is positive psychology, which emphasizes human strengths and virtues to promote well-being. The work of Dr. Martin Seligman, the founder of positive psychology, has identified various factors that contribute to happiness, such as positive emotions, engagement, relationships, meaning, and accomplishment. His research has led to the development of interventions and techniques that can assist individuals in cultivating these factors to enhance their overall well-being.

Scientific research offers invaluable insights into the complexities of happiness and human experience. As we persist in exploring the countless factors contributing to happiness, we enrich our understanding of how our experiences, beliefs, and memories shape our perceptions of well-being. From the impact of transformative journeys and the influence of nature on our mental health, to the pliability of memory and the fundamental principles of positive psychology, each study adds another piece to the complex puzzle of happiness.

These findings paint a vivid portrait, revealing the profound influence of experiences on long-term satisfaction, as well as the subtle deception of hedonic adaptation. While cautioning against the ephemeral nature of initial happiness, the studies illuminate the enduring impact of experiences over material possessions, forging a connection to our sense of self and social bonds. As we navigate the labyrinth of memory, we confront its fallibility and the skewed lens through which we perceive our past. Yet, amidst the twists and turns, the embrace of nature and the guiding principles of positive psychology offer beacons of hope. Through their wisdom, we uncover the intricate pieces that shape our understanding of happiness—how experiences, beliefs, and memories intertwine to create our unique perception of well-being.

Part IV

Unveiling Happiness's Hidden Layers

Chapter XI

Brewing Happiness and The Power of Experience Stretching

Imagine yourself in a familiar coffee shop, savouring a sip of your usual Americano. Suddenly, the taste explodes on your palate - a blend of darkness, bitterness, and pure delight. It's as if this ordinary coffee has been transformed into an extraordinary experience. This phenomenon is known as 'experience stretching.'

From a young age, we are conditioned to believe that more experiences lead to greater happiness. But recent research challenges this assumption. Studies suggest that individuals with fewer emotional encounters tend to experience emotions with greater intensity when they do arise.

Think of a child tasting chocolate for the first time. It's an explosion of sweetness and pleasure, an entirely novel sensation that sets a high standard for future chocolate experiences. This is the essence of 'experience stretching' at play.

Now, consider another intriguing finding. People who have faced adversity often find more joy and happiness in life compared to those who have had smoother journeys. It seems that sailing through storms enhances our appreciation for the calm seas. The narrowness or challenges within our experiences can, unexpectedly, enrich our happiness.

So, how can we ensure we cultivate the right experiences? How can we nurture a perspective that stretches our happiness? Mindfulness and gratitude hold significant importance.

Studies show that individuals who incorporate gratitude into their daily lives tend to experience more positive emotions, higher life satisfaction, and fewer episodes of depression.

Similarly, practising mindfulness through activities like meditation and deep breathing exercises can contribute to increased happiness and satisfaction with life.

Therefore, the next time you relish your coffee or indulge in a piece of chocolate, remember the concept of 'experience stretching.' Happiness isn't solely about the quantity of our experiences but the quality and perspective we bring to them. And always remember, there is no definitive recipe for happiness - each person has the power to brew their own unique blend.

Chapter XII

The Complexities of Happiness in Extreme Situations

In 1972, a plane carrying a Uruguayan rugby team crashed in the Andes mountains, leaving the survivors stranded without food or proper clothing. After months of struggle and loss, a group of survivors hiked for ten days through the treacherous mountains to find help. Despite the unimaginable circumstances they faced, some of the survivors described feeling a sense of purpose and even joy during their journey. This raises the question of whether we can understand and evaluate another person's happiness in extreme situations, and how subjective experiences can be. This phenomenon is not unique to the Andes survivors, and research has been conducted to explore the complexities of happiness in extreme situations.

A study published in the journal "Nature" in 2016, conducted by a team of researchers led by neuroscientist David Eagleman, sought to explore how subjective experiences can be in extreme situations. The researchers asked participants to rate their subjective experiences while undergoing various tasks, including holding their hands in ice-cold water and being pushed out of a plane during a skydive. The study found that individuals who were pushed out of a plane reported feeling significantly happier after the experience than those who held their hands in the ice-cold water, despite the fact that both experiences were physically and emotionally taxing. This research suggests that even in situations that are objectively negative, subjective experiences can vary greatly, making it difficult to understand and evaluate another person's happiness.

Another study published in the journal "Frontiers in Psychology" in 2018, led by psychologist Frank Martela, sought to explore the concept of "post-traumatic growth" - the idea that individuals can experience personal growth and positive changes after experiencing trauma or adversity. The study surveyed individuals who had experienced a wide range of traumatic events, including war, natural disasters, and personal loss. The results showed that many individuals reported experiencing positive changes, including a greater sense of purpose and appreciation for life, after their traumatic experiences. This research suggests that happiness can be found even in the most challenging and traumatic situations, and that individuals may experience personal growth and positive changes as a result of these experiences.

Similarly, a study published in the journal "Psychology and Aging" in 2013, led by psychologist Laura Carstensen, explored the idea of "socio emotional selectivity" - the concept that as individuals age, they prioritize emotional experiences over material ones. The study found that older adults reported feeling happier and more satisfied with their lives than younger adults, despite facing a variety of challenges associated with aging, such as declining health and social isolation. This research suggests that happiness can be found in different ways throughout the lifespan, and that subjective experiences of happiness may change over time.

However, it is important to note that subjective experiences of happiness can also be influenced by factors such as personality traits and cultural values. A study published in the journal "Emotion" in 2015, led by psychologist Shigehiro Oishi, explored how cultural values can influence subjective experiences of happiness. The study compared individuals from two different cultural backgrounds - one that emphasized individualism and personal achievement, and one that emphasized collectivism and social harmony. The results showed that individuals from the collectivistic culture reported feeling happier when they were able to meet their social obligations and maintain harmonious relationships with others, while individuals from the individualistic culture reported feeling happier when they achieved personal goals and experienced individual success. This research suggests that cultural values can shape subjective experiences of happiness, highlighting the importance of understanding cultural differences when evaluating another person's happiness.

A 2015 study in "Emotion" by Shigehiro Oishi compared happiness between individualistic and collectivistic cultures. It's similar to the difference between my friend Leah, who enjoys the sense of achievement from completing a marathon, and my friend Hiroshi, who finds joy in family gatherings. Oishi found that individualists were happier when they achieved personal goals, while collectivists found happiness in meeting social obligations and maintaining harmony with others. This shows how cultural factors can shape our perception of happiness.

These studies offer profound insights into the intricate nature of happiness and subjective experiences.

They reveal that extreme circumstances can challenge our understanding of happiness, as subjective experiences vary greatly even in the face of adversity. This complexity highlights the difficulty in accurately evaluating another person's happiness. Moreover, the findings demonstrate that traumatic experiences can spark personal growth and positive changes, shedding light on the potential for happiness amidst challenges. The passage of time brings forth a shift in priorities, with older adults valuing emotional experiences and reporting higher levels of happiness and life satisfaction. Cultural values also play a significant role, shaping the subjective experiences of happiness. Individualistic cultures emphasize personal achievements, while collectivistic cultures find happiness in meeting social obligations and fostering harmony. In grasping the intricacies of happiness, we must consider individual differences, situational factors, and cultural influences. Thus, these studies illuminate the multidimensional tapestry of happiness and emphasize the need for a nuanced understanding of subjective experiences.

Chapter XIII

Unconscious Influence on Conscious Experience

The unique tapestry of human existence is undeniably intricately woven with threads of our experiences. These experiences not only anchor our understanding of the world around us but also sculpt our perception of reality. Conventionally, it is assumed that there exists an inseparable link between experience and consciousness, asserting that our consciousness directly engenders our experiences. However, ground-breaking scientific revelations propose that this presupposition may not necessarily align with the truth.

A myriad of scientific studies, particularly within the realm of neuroscience, have underscored the existence of a significant part of our experiences occurring outside the purview of our conscious awareness. For instance, an intriguing domain of research is the study of visual perception. It has been discovered that the conscious mind is privy to only a minuscule fraction of the visual information processed by our brains. Despite our brains being incessantly inundated with a deluge of visual data, our awareness remains limited to a certain amount of this data at any given moment. This intriguing observation implies that our experiences are not strictly born out of our consciousness but rather are a product of unconscious processes pervading our brains.

In alignment with this is another fascinating field of study – memory. Numerous studies have highlighted that substantial learning and memory formation transpire outside of our conscious awareness. A notable instance of this is a study conducted by a team of researchers at the University of California, San Diego. They found that participants exposed to a specific sound during sleep demonstrated an enhanced ability to recall information learned while awake. The conclusion drawn from the study was that the sound stimulus was processed by the participants' brains during sleep, which subsequently led to improved memory retention.

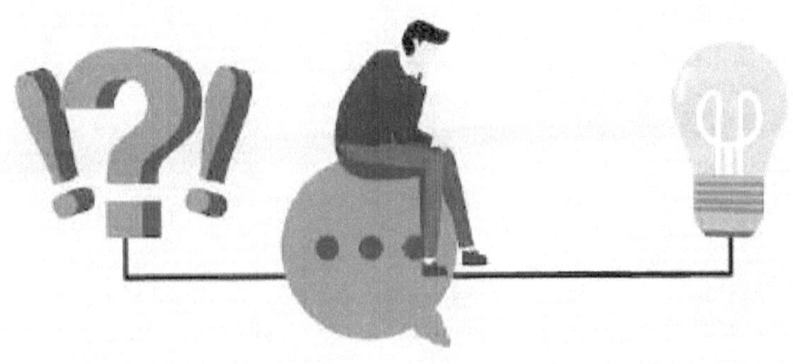

Such revelations suggest a paradigm shift in understanding our experiences – as not merely the offspring of our conscious awareness, but rather the result of a sophisticated interplay between conscious and unconscious processes within our brains. This newfound understanding carries profound implications for our interpretation of the world around us.

One noteworthy implication of this is the possibility of our exposure to experiences of which we are not consciously aware. To illustrate, an individual may encounter a specific odor or sound that triggers a potent emotional response, notwithstanding their lack of conscious awareness of the stimulus. This premise indicates that our experiences extend beyond the boundaries of our conscious awareness, suggesting a more profound and intricate process operating within our minds.

Furthermore, it also implies that our experiences may be subtly swayed by factors unbeknownst to our conscious mind. A compelling instance of this is a study led by a group of researchers at the University of Amsterdam. The study found that participants exposed to a particular odor while engaged in a task were subsequently more inclined to opt for a product associated with the scent. The conclusion inferred from this study was that the participants' decision-making process was unconsciously influenced by the odor.

These discoveries present a series of compelling inquiries about the true nature of experience and consciousness. If we can indeed have experiences outside our conscious awareness, what does it signify about the nature of our experiences? Are our experiences genuinely subjective, or are they shaped by hidden processes within our brains? Moreover, if our experiences are subtly influenced by factors outside our conscious awareness, what implications does it carry for our ability to make independent and uninfluenced decisions? Do we truly hold the reins of our experiences, or are they manipulated by elements beyond our conscious control?

Happiness, that elusive state of being, appears to be more intricate than meets the eye. Recent scientific findings challenge the notion that our conscious experiences hold sole dominion over our joyous existence. Neuroscience reveals a clandestine world of unconscious influence, where our perception of reality and emotional responses are woven by hidden threads. Visual perception studies disclose that our conscious mind merely grazes the surface of the visual feast our brains consume. Memory formation, too, occurs behind the veils of consciousness, with sounds infiltrating our slumber to enhance recall. This paradigm shift uncovers the enigmatic interplay between the conscious and unconscious, suggesting that our experiences extend beyond the boundaries of awareness. Our happiness, it seems, dances to the tune of subtle influences unbeknownst to our conscious minds. Yet, as research delves deeper, the answers to the mysteries of happiness beckon, promising a richer understanding of the human psyche and the true nature of joy.

Part V

Exploring the Dimensions of Happiness

Chapter XIV

Measuring the Immeasurable and Navigating the Subjectivity of Happiness

Rene Descartes, a celebrated mathematician and philosopher, propounded that our personal experiences provide the only certainty in our ever-changing world. But does this assertion hold when we try to comprehend a concept as nebulous as happiness? Can it be that the scientific probing into subjective experiences, including emotions, is even more challenging and complex than we dare to imagine? Amidst this sea of daunting inquiries, there shines a beacon of optimism. We can bridge this metaphorical gap in comprehension, provided we are ready to accept three fundamental assumptions. Brace yourself for a riveting journey that will question the very essence of scientific principles, dive deep into the process of quantifying the unquantifiable, and commence a pursuit of uncovering the true nature of happiness.

We initiate our journey with Descartes' proposition. Famously known for his philosophical axiom "Cogito, ergo sum" translating to "I think, therefore I am," Descartes argued that our individual experiences constitute the foundation of our certainty in the world. However, when this principle is applied to happiness, the clarity begins to fade. Numerous scientific investigations have ventured into the labyrinth of human emotion, attempting to quantify and comprehend its intricacies.

For example, research in positive psychology has made attempts to measure happiness. A landmark study conducted by the University of California, Berkeley, utilized functional magnetic resonance imaging (fMRI) to identify brain regions associated with feelings of joy and satisfaction. While these studies are revolutionary, they also expose the inherent subjectivity and variability of happiness. The way happiness is experienced varies greatly from one individual to another. This inherent subjectivity poses a significant challenge in establishing a universal standard for happiness or any other subjective experience.

The intricacy of scientifically studying subjective experiences is further underscored by research into memory and recollection. Cognitive psychologist Elizabeth Loftus, through her work on the misinformation effect, demonstrated that our memories are not rigid, but flexible, and can be influenced by incorrect information. This suggests that even our memory of joyful experiences may not be entirely precise, adding an additional layer of complexity to the understanding and measurement of happiness.

Nevertheless, amidst these challenges, a glimmer of optimism persists. Although it might appear as a Herculean task, the gap in our understanding can be bridged by accepting three essential premises: the subjectivity of happiness, the ability of science to adjust its methods to study the unmeasurable, and the importance of interdisciplinary approaches.

Firstly, we need to accept that happiness is an intensely personal and subjective experience. Just as an artist perceives a range of hues where others see a single colour, each individual experiences happiness in their unique manner. This premise opens the door to a more refined approach to studying happiness, one that accepts variability as an integral part of the process.

Secondly, it's critical to acknowledge that while science is founded on empirical evidence and quantification, it's also a discipline that continually evolves and adapts. The emergence of qualitative research methods, such as narrative analysis and phenomenology, showcases science's capacity to delve into experiences that are seemingly unquantifiable.

Lastly, an interdisciplinary approach is essential in unravelling the enigma of happiness. Happiness is a complex phenomenon that encompasses psychological, physiological, social, and cultural dimensions. By integrating knowledge and perspectives from various fields such as psychology, neuroscience, sociology, and philosophy, we can construct a more comprehensive understanding of happiness and its determinants.

In conclusion, the study of happiness poses unique challenges due to its subjective nature and the limitations of scientific measurement. However, by embracing the subjectivity of happiness, adapting scientific methods to capture its nuances, and fostering interdisciplinary collaboration, we can gradually uncover the secrets of happiness and deepen our comprehension of this elusive yet essential aspect of human existence.

Chapter XV

Probing Happiness' Elusive Depths

The complexities of happiness and fulfilment are exemplified by two real-life figures: Malala Yousafzai and Robin Williams. Their stories challenge our understanding of happiness and success, urging us to explore the intricacies of the human mind and the impact of adversity.

Malala Yousafzai, a Pakistani activist, faced unimaginable adversity when she was targeted by the Taliban for advocating girls' education. Surviving a vicious assassination attempt, she could have succumbed to despair. However, Malala's resilience and determination shone through. She transformed her pain into a driving force, becoming a global advocate for education rights. Through her unwavering commitment, Malala found fulfilment and joy in empowering others, despite the hardships she endured.

On the other hand, Robin Williams, a beloved comedian and actor, battled with depression despite his immense success in the entertainment industry. His talent brought laughter and happiness to millions, but behind the scenes, he struggled with profound sadness. Despite his ability to bring joy to others, Williams found it difficult to find happiness within himself. Tragically, his inner demons led him to a tragic end, reminding us that even those who seemingly have it all can grapple with deep emotional pain.

The stories of Malala and Robin Williams highlight the complexities of happiness and success. They demonstrate that external achievements and circumstances do not always guarantee inner fulfilment. True happiness often lies in finding purpose, making a positive impact, and nurturing our mental and emotional well-being, regardless of the adversities we face.

These examples challenge our preconceived notions and urge us to examine the intricacies of human happiness. They remind us that happiness cannot be measured solely by external achievements, but rather by the resilience, purpose, and inner contentment we cultivate within ourselves. These accounts of Malala and Robin underscore the profound paradox of human happiness and success. They challenge our assumptions about what constitutes happiness and fulfilment and the paths we choose to reach these states. In our pursuit of happiness, we often rely on our memory, perception, and imagination to guide our decisions. We build scenarios in our minds, predicting how certain outcomes will make us feel. But what if our cognitive processes are flawed?

Scientific research into human cognition suggests that our mental faculties, while impressive, are not infallible. Memory, for instance, is prone to distortions and inaccuracies. Studies have shown that our recollections can be influenced by subsequent information, leading to the phenomenon known as "misinformation effect." Perception, too, is susceptible to various biases. Research in cognitive psychology has identified numerous perceptual biases, like the confirmation bias, which leads us to favour information that confirms our pre-existing beliefs.

Similarly, our ability to imagine future scenarios, known as prospect ion, can be flawed. Our minds tend to overestimate the intensity and duration of future emotional reactions, a bias known as "affective forecasting error." Moreover, research suggests that we often fail to consider how our future selves will change over time, leading us to make decisions that our future selves may not agree with, a phenomenon known as "end of history illusion."

These cognitive quirks and biases can lead us to make misjudgements about what will bring us happiness and fulfilment, leading to potential errors in decision-making. Could it be that our perceptions of happiness and fulfilment are influenced by these cognitive biases? Might we be misjudging our paths to happiness based on faulty mental simulations? Turing's steadfastness amidst adversity and Hughes' struggle despite his success suggest that our predictions about happiness might be far from accurate.

Research into human cognition and decision-making lends weight to this theory. For instance, a study published in the Journal of Personality and Social Psychology found that people's predictions about how different outcomes would affect their happiness were often incorrect. Participants overestimated how much a positive or negative event would impact their overall happiness, pointing towards the limitations of our imagination in predicting our future emotional states.

In another study published in science, researchers found that people often misremember past experiences, focusing more on the peak and end moments of an event rather than the entirety of the experience. This "peak-end rule" suggests that our memories, too, are imperfect guides for our decision-making, further complicating our quest for happiness.

When it comes to perception, we know from cognitive psychology that our brains are wired to notice certain things while ignoring others, a phenomenon known as selective attention. This can distort our view of the present, leading us to overlook potential sources of happiness right in front of us. Furthermore, we are susceptible to various cognitive biases that can lead us to make incorrect assessments about our current state of happiness, such as the "focusing illusion," which is the tendency to overestimate the impact of one aspect of a situation on the overall outcome.

Taking these findings into account, it becomes clear that our ability to accurately predict, remember, and perceive happiness is fraught with challenges. Our brains, while incredibly powerful, are not infallible and can lead us astray in our quest for happiness and fulfilment. These cognitive quirks can lead us to make decisions that seem right at the time but might not lead to the happiness we anticipate.

So, when we look at the stories of Malala and Robin, we must ask ourselves: Are our predictions about what will bring us happiness accurate? Or are we prone to a fundamental miscalculation, a cognitive fallacy, in our pursuit of happiness? Unravelling this paradox requires us to delve deeper into the inner workings of the human brain and the elusive mechanisms governing our emotions and decisions. As we seek to understand the complexities of human happiness, we may find that our preconceptions about success and fulfilment need to be re-evaluated.

Chapter XVI

Weaving the Memory Web

The human brain's ability to store a seemingly infinite amount of information, from the banal to the profound, is truly astounding. But what are the intricacies behind our brain's ability to weave a tapestry of our experiences, all while not reaching its storage capacity? The answer lies in the labyrinth of memory formation, storage, and recall - the science of memory.

The human brain exhibits an incredible ability to store vast quantities of data through a multitude of mechanisms. Memory consolidation is one key method in which our brain accomplishes this. It's a process where short-term memories transition to long-term memories, ready to be accessed and retrieved at a later time.

Indeed, our brains are incessantly at work consolidating memories, even in our sleep. An example of this is a study by the University of Bristol, which discovered the pivotal role

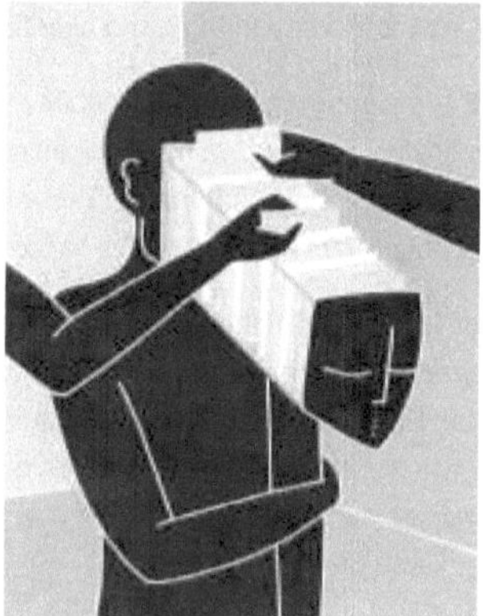

sleep plays in consolidating spatial memories. Participants who napped after a spatial memory task were found to perform significantly better when retested, compared to those who didn't nap.

But memory consolidation isn't the sole player in this memory game. Schemas, mental structures that help us comprehend and organize information, are also fundamental. They enable us to categorize information more efficiently, aiding in the swift and precise retrieval of memories.

A fascinating feature of our memory system is the brain's capacity to fabricate information during memory recall. Elizabeth Loftus and her team at the University of California, Irvine, demonstrated this through a study where participants were shown a deceptive photo of a stop sign with a yield sign in the background. Many participants later claimed to remember seeing a yield sign at the intersection, though none was present. This phenomenon, known as the misinformation effect, underscores the importance of acknowledging the limitations of our memory and its susceptibility to external influences.

Arguably, the most enthralling aspect of the memory system is the brain's ability to intertwine our experiences into a tapestry of memories. Memories are not a mere compilation of isolated events and facts, but rather an interconnected narrative. This construction of a coherent narrative from our experiences is known as memory integration.

Without memory integration, our memories would resemble a jumbled collection of fragments. Mental maps, which assist in organizing and connecting disparate experiences and events, have been shown to facilitate memory integration. For instance, researchers at the University of Pennsylvania found that individuals recalling a personal event were more likely to remember the event in the context of other events happening around the same time. This indicates that our brains utilize mental maps to weave our experiences into a coherent narrative.

Memory integration isn't confined to individual experiences; it also transpires on a larger scale. A study by the University of Illinois at Urbana-Champaign showed that people who had experienced a significant historical event, such as the 9/11 terrorist attacks, were likely to incorporate their personal memories of the event into the broader cultural narrative. This synthesis of personal and cultural memories is crucial for developing a shared sense of history and identity.

Moreover, memory integration illuminates the significance of storytelling and narrative in our lives. Our memories aren't just facts and events but are filled with meaning and significance through the narratives we weave. A study by the University of North Carolina at Chapel Hill found that participants who narrated a story about a personal event recalled the event's details better than those who merely recounted the facts. This finding suggests that constructing narratives around our experiences helps us understand and integrate them into our larger life story.

The complex landscape of memory, with its intertwining processes of consolidation, schema formation, and memory integration, offers a fascinating glimpse into the workings of the human brain and the essence of human experience. As we continue to delve into the intricacies of memory, we will undoubtedly uncover more about the complex relationship between perception, cognition, and identity.

Through a deeper understanding of the mechanisms underlying our memory system, we may also devise novel ways to enhance memory function and boost overall cognitive performance.

In delving into the intricate workings of memory, we uncover profound insights that challenge our assumptions about happiness. Our memories, while awe-inspiring, are not the reliable record keepers we often perceive them to be. They are susceptible to biases, distortions, and the sway of external influences. Understanding the fallibility of our memory encourages a healthy scepticism, prompting us to question the accuracy of our recollections. Moreover, the integration of memories into a cohesive narrative emerges as a powerful force shaping our sense of identity and our perception of the world. Crafting meaningful narratives around our experiences becomes a gateway to enhancing our ability to recall details and infusing our lives with purpose and fulfilment. By embracing the complexities of memory and its profound impact on our emotions and personal growth, we unlock a deeper understanding of the intricate interplay between memory and happiness.

Part VI

Unraveling the Mysteries of the Human Mind

Chapter XVII

Analysis of the Brain's Ability to Fill Information Gaps

Our brain, a marvel of nature, serves as the command centre that deciphers the complex sensory data we encounter, enabling us to comprehend our environment. It artfully integrates numerous sensory stimuli with cognitive functions to construct our perception of the world, painting a comprehensive picture from seemingly fragmented information.

One of the brain's most intriguing attributes is its adeptness at interpolating missing data. Imagine walking down a bustling city street, suddenly noticing a void in your field of vision. Astoundingly, our brain doesn't leave this area blank. Instead, it concocts details to render a continuous visual panorama. This ingenious 'filling-in' phenomenon is not exclusive to vision; research shows our brain can also 'hear' absent sounds or words, showcasing its versatility.

Pioneering scientific research has underscored the critical role of this filling-in mechanism in our perception. A paradigmatic experiment demonstrates this beautifully: participants were presented a series of letters, with one conspicuously absent. Yet, they correctly identified the word, suggesting their brains interpolated the missing data. Similar auditory tests revealed this ability isn't confined to the visual realm; participants could 'hear' absent sounds and words, highlighting the brain's multidimensional processing power.

However, this interpolative function isn't restricted to straightforward tasks like letter or sound identification. Our brain also extrapolates from our past experiences and expectations to create a coherent image of our environment. For instance, if we glimpse a fragment of a recognizable object - say, a car - our brain assembles the missing parts based on our past experiences and knowledge of cars. In situations where sensory input is ambiguous or incomplete, such as a dimly lit scene, our brain applies our expectations to interpolate missing data.

That said, this remarkable ability is not infallible. Occasionally, our brain might interpolate data inaccurately. Suppose we perceive a part of a familiar object, and our brain interpolates the missing pieces. In this case, we might end up with a skewed perception of the object. Similarly, if our brain fills in a missing word, it could create a false memory of the conversation.

Appreciating the mechanics of the brain's filling-in ability might shatter the illusion of seamless perception. Still, our brains are programmed to trust their interpretations, even when they deviate from reality. This is because the filling-in mechanism is integral to our perception, and without it, our perception would be disjointed and incomplete.

This leads us to an intriguing question: how much of our perception is real, and how much is a product of our brain's creative license? The answer isn't clear-cut, hinging on the specific context and the ambiguity level of the sensory input. In some scenarios, our brain's interpolative ability may yield a perception almost identical to the actual sensory input. In contrast, in other situations, our brain may conjure up a perception that deviates significantly from reality. Despite its imperfections, our brain's filling-in ability is crucial to our perception, enabling us to construct a continuous image of our surroundings despite inherent gaps in our sensory input.

Moreover, comprehending the constraints of our brain's filling-in ability has practical applications across disciplines. In design and marketing, leveraging this knowledge can facilitate the creation of compelling visuals that evoke the desired perception or emotion. In healthcare, understanding this mechanism can equip medical professionals to better diagnose and treat conditions impacting perception, such as visual or auditory impairments.

Our brain's interpolative function allows us to construct a coherent and continuous image of the world, even when faced with incomplete or ambiguous sensory input. This mechanism demonstrates the brain's adaptability and its reliance on past experiences and expectations to create a seamless perception. However, it's important to recognize that this ability is not infallible, and our brain's interpretations can sometimes deviate from reality. By appreciating the limitations of our perception and the potential for inaccuracies, we can approach happiness with a sense of openness and flexibility. Understanding that our perception is a dynamic and subjective construction enables us to cultivate a more nuanced and resilient perspective on life, embracing the imperfections and uncertainties that come with it.

Chapter XVIII

The Marvel and Pitfalls of Predictive Thinking

Imagination is a vital component of our cognitive architecture, yet it often goes unnoticed due to its effortless and automatic operation. Our brains weave images and scenarios in our mental theatre without our conscious direction. However, this ease of generation can be a double-edged sword, leading us down paths of illusion rather than accurate prediction.

As we craft mental narratives, our minds incorporate details from our personal experiences and predispositions, painting a vivid and specific tableau. This process, while fascinating, can potentially misguide us when we attempt to anticipate our responses to prospective events, as our predictions hinge on the details our minds have autonomously generated. To illustrate this point, let's consider a scientific experiment involving the mental visualization of a spaghetti meal for dinner. When presented with this idea, your brain spontaneously manifests a specific image - maybe a generous mound of pasta drenched in a hearty Bolognese sauce served at your cherished restaurant. Subsequently, you speculate your level of satisfaction from this meal, drawing from this detailed cerebral illustration. However, the notion of "spaghetti for dinner" is a broad concept and can symbolize a multitude of variations. Your forecast of enjoyment is swayed by the particular version you've mentally constructed, possibly leading to inaccurate predictions if the real-world experience deviates from your mental depiction.

This proclivity to envisage the future, influenced by the mind's automatic detail-filling, pervades beyond just forecasting our reactions to mundane pleasures like food. It permeates our anticipations of transformative life events as well. Our brains, functioning akin to artists colouring a sketch, can potentially distort the true scenario, steering us towards flawed predictions about our emotional responses to future circumstances.

For instance, in another scientific study exploring the psychology of future thinking, participants were asked to predict their emotional reactions to a range of scenarios, from social events like parties to more personal situations such as losing a job or receiving a promotion. The results showed that people often overestimate their emotional reactions to these future events, both positive and negative. This illustrates the gap between our imaginative capabilities and our predictive accuracy.

Our minds possess the remarkable ability to construct intricate, detailed images with little conscious effort. This talent for imagination is truly a marvel of human cognition. However, we must keep in mind that these details are often mental fabrications, not precise reflections of reality. Recognizing this can safeguard us from misestimation the emotional outcomes of future occurrences.

So, what can we do to navigate this complex landscape of human experience more accurately? First and foremost, we must be mindful of our tendency to rely on mental fabrications when making predictions. We must recognize that our imaginative capabilities do not always equate to predictive accuracy. Second, we can strive to broaden our perspectives and consider multiple variations of a given scenario, rather than fixating on a single mental depiction. By doing so, we can increase the likelihood of more accurate predictions and reduce the risk of disappointment or surprise when faced with reality.

In conclusion, imagination is a powerful tool that is deeply intertwined with our cognitive architecture.

While it can be a source of marvel and wonder, it can also lead us astray when used for predictive thinking. By recognizing the limitations of our imaginative minds and broadening our perspectives, we can navigate the complex landscape of human experience more accurately.

Chapter XIX

The Intricate Machinations of the Human Brain

As we stand on the brink of understanding the inception of human life, the birthplace of existence itself, we find ourselves endowed with the formidable power to select the design of our brain. This possibility is both exhilarating and daunting. Thankfully, nature did not burden us with such a decision, bestowing upon us brains of unparalleled complexity, systems of intricate networks offering an array of functionalities that no other organ can match.

Our brains possess the unique ability to complete the incomplete, to fill the gaps in our perceptions, ensuring that our memory and imagination aren't fragmented or lacking. However, this extraordinary cognitive ability, while preserving the coherence of our reality, has its price. It can lead us astray, into the realm of perceiving entities that don't exist, remembering incidents that never took place, and predicting the future based on our imaginative conjectures. This exciting journey into the maze of the human mind raises a question: What important details could our brains be leaving out?

Scientific research has played a key role in revealing how our brains create a smooth and continuous reality. Neuroscience, for instance, has demonstrated how our brains use a "filling-in" mechanism to handle missing or incomplete data in our sensory experiences. The blind spot in our vision is a prime example of this cognitive phenomenon, where our brain creates missing details to provide a continuous visual experience. Similarly, it assists in connecting fragmented memories and fostering a vibrant imagination, thus maintaining the integrity of our perceptions.

However, this extraordinary ability is not without its drawbacks. It can lead us to perceive things that don't exist, scientifically known as pareidolia, where our minds detect patterns or similarities in random stimuli. Seeing faces in clouds or interpreting messages in white noise are typical examples of pareidolia. The brain's filling-in mechanism can also affect our memory, leading us to remember events that didn't happen. This cognitive distortion, known as false memory, can be so convincing that we staunchly defend the truth of these non-existent events.

Another intriguing aspect of the brain's functionality is its ability to project the future. The brain's capacity to imagine, plan, and predict the future is largely based on its ability to integrate past experiences and current stimuli. However, our imaginative predictions of the future are not always accurate. This is evident in 'affective forecasting', where individuals often misjudge their future emotional states, leading to errors in decision-making.

As we journey further into the enigmatic maze of the human brain, we are faced with a captivating question: What essential details might our brains be hiding from us? The brain's filling-in mechanism, while providing a unified reality, might be leaving out crucial details from our perceptions. Some scientific studies suggest that our brains selectively filter out redundant or irrelevant information to avoid cognitive overload. This 'selective attention' allows us to concentrate on relevant details and disregard unnecessary distractions.

However, the compromise is that we might miss out on essential information in our surroundings. For instance, in the famous 'invisible gorilla' experiment, participants engrossed in a task didn't notice a person in a gorilla suit walking across the screen. This example of 'inattentional blindness' is a stark reminder of the potential limitations of our perception.

The human brain, a complex and captivating organ, enables us to experience the world around us in a seamless and consistent manner. However, its abilities and strategies come with a cost, potentially leading to errors and distortions in our perceptions and memories. Through scientific research, we can gain a better understanding of the brain's mechanisms and apply this knowledge to improve our lives and address neurological and mental health challenges.

Part VII

Love, Life, and Emotional Intelligence

Chapter XX

Unlocking the Mystery of Romantic Chemistry

In the grand tapestry of human emotion, love, with its intoxicating allure and mysterious depths, has long been a source of fascination for poets, philosophers, and scientists alike. As we embark on this exploration, we'll delve into the intricate dance of neurobiology and psychology that underpins our universal experience of love. By peering through the scientific lens at romantic love, we hope to illuminate how it shapes our happiness and overall well-being. We will unearth that the roots of love are woven deeply into the very fabric of our brain chemistry, orchestrated by a mesmerizing symphony of neurotransmitters such as dopamine, oxytocin, and serotonin.

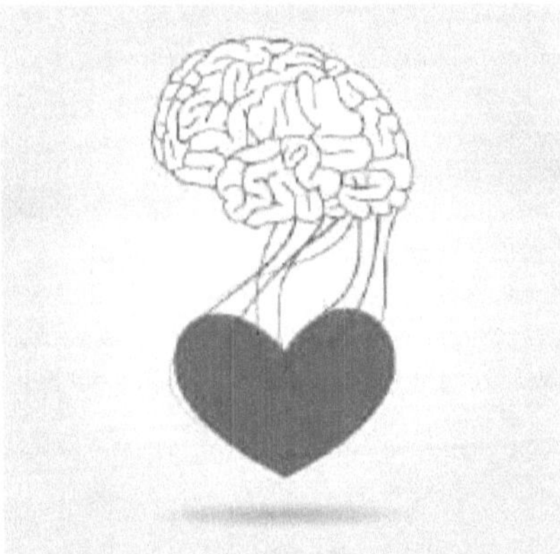

First off, let's unravel the role of these neurotransmitters in the complex ballet of romantic attraction and attachment. Our brain, a wonder of nature's architecture, communicates via an elaborate network of neurons. These neurons, in their turn, use neurotransmitters as chemical couriers, dispatching signals that shape our thoughts, emotions, and behaviours.

The star of the show, dopamine, is the so-called "reward chemical," taking centre stage in the experience of love. It's closely linked to feelings of bliss, motivation, and reward, bursting forth in response to pleasurable experiences. Within the theatre of love, dopamine showers our brain during pleasurable moments with our partner, from the simple act of hand-holding to more intimate rendezvous. This dopamine deluge amplifies these pleasurable experiences and drives us to seek them out again, acting as a kind of internal rewards program. Dopamine, therefore, is the key player behind that heady sense of joy and exhilaration often associated with the early stages of a romance.

Next up, we encounter oxytocin, fittingly dubbed the "love hormone." This neurotransmitter has a starring role in the creation and sustenance of close interpersonal bonds. Oxytocin is released during physical touch and intimacy, engendering profound feelings of bonding and attachment. Studies show that higher oxytocin levels correlate with a greater sense of emotional intimacy and attachment security in couples, underscoring its vital role in the commitment phase of a romantic relationship. Oxytocin nurtures our ability to trust and connect with others, laying the groundwork for a healthy and loving relationship.

Rounding out our trio of neurotransmitters is serotonin, a major player in our mood and overall well-being. Its deficiency has been tied to conditions such as depression and anxiety, while its presence contributes to feelings of happiness and satisfaction. In the realm of love, serotonin levels can colour our perception of romantic partners. Research shows that during the initial phases of falling in love, serotonin levels can dip, echoing the levels seen in individuals with Obsessive-Compulsive Disorder. This might explain why those in the early stages of love often Harbour obsessive thoughts about their partner.

The dance between these neurotransmitters paints a vibrant picture of how our brain chemistry influences our experiences and perceptions of romantic love. However, it's important to note that the biological processes are just one side of the coin. Falling in love also involves complex psychological processes, such as cognitive appraisal, emotional responses, and behavioural reactions. It touches our self-concept, emotions, and social interactions, ultimately shaping our mental well-being.

Now, let's illustrate the dance of neurobiological and psychological processes in the context of romantic love with some examples.

John and Emma, two art lovers, first met at a local gallery. Despite their differing personalities—John, the extrovert, and Emma, the introvert—they were instantly drawn to each other. This initial connection can be chalked up to the principle of similarity. Their shared love for art and shared values enhanced understanding and communication, laying the groundwork for their burgeoning relationship.

As their relationship blossomed, the release of neurotransmitters like dopamine began to shape their shared experiences. Memorable dates and shared moments triggered a dopamine rush, amplifying the pleasure and reward associated with their time together, thus heightening their desire to seek more such experiences.

As their bond deepened, oxytocin also made its entrance. Physical touch, like holding hands or sharing a hug, triggered the release of this 'love hormone', further solidifying their bond and fostering a sense of attachment. This emotional intimacy nurtured a strong sense of trust and security in their relationship.

On the psychological front, their ability to communicate effectively played a key role in maintaining their connection. Openly sharing thoughts, dreams, and fears fostered a deeper understanding, strengthening their emotional bond, and offering a haven for vulnerability.

In another love story, David and Lisa, despite their contrasting personalities, felt an immediate connection at a friend's gathering. Their relationship story can be understood through the principle of proximity. Living in the same building, they frequently crossed paths, which led to increased interaction and familiarity, and subsequently, the blossoming of their relationship.

As their relationship matured, they too experienced the rush and ebb of neurotransmitters. Exciting adventures together, like exploring new places or trying novel activities, triggered a surge of dopamine, enhancing their pleasure and excitement, reinforcing their bond, and creating lasting memories.

The course of their relationship wasn't always smooth sailing, but their commitment to effective conflict resolution helped them navigate through these challenges. By approaching conflicts with an openness to understanding each other's perspectives and finding compromises, they maintained a healthy emotional environment and reinforced their commitment to each other.

In both these love stories, the interplay between neurobiology and psychology steered the course of the relationships. The release of neurotransmitters like dopamine and oxytocin fostered feelings of pleasure, reward, bonding, and attachment. Meanwhile, psychological aspects like effective communication and conflict resolution nurtured understanding, trust, and commitment.

These examples underscore how the intricate interplay of neurobiology and psychology shapes our experiences of romantic love, highlighting the multifaceted nature of this universal human phenomenon.

Let us delve into the captivating realm of attraction, where we unravel the intricate dynamics of mate selection. Within this realm, physical attractiveness holds undeniable influence. Universally appealing features, like symmetrical facial structures, clear skin, and signs of good health, draw our attention. Even infants as young as three months old are instinctively attracted to attractive faces, suggesting a hardwired preference that carries into adulthood.

Body proportions also play a significant role in our assessment of attractiveness. The universally desirable "hourglass" figure, with a slender waist and wider hips, consistently appeals to both men and women across cultures. This preference reflects an innate recognition of reproductive potential and has stood the test of time.

Scent-based attraction, operating through pheromones, adds another layer to the complexities of mate selection. Pheromones are chemical signals that can trigger physiological and behavioural responses in others. Although the specific pheromones and mechanisms involved are not fully understood, research indicates that scent can influence attraction and mate preference, potentially conveying information about genetic compatibility and reproductive fitness.

Non-verbal communication serves as a powerful medium for expressing attraction and interest. Non-verbal cues like a genuine smile, direct eye contact, and an open body posture have consistently been associated with attractiveness and positive social perceptions. These cues communicate approachability, confidence, and a genuine desire to connect, playing a pivotal role in initial attraction and the development of relationships.

Voice pitch, too, weaves its enchanting spell in the realm of attraction. Men and women are naturally drawn to voices that hint at high reproductive potential. Women tend to find men with lower-pitched voices more attractive, perceiving them as possessing greater genetic benefits. Conversely, men are often attracted to higher-pitched voices in women, which are associated with youthfulness and femininity. Voice pitch can significantly impact initial attraction and the mate selection process.

The intricate dynamics of attraction, with its interplay of physical beauty, scent, non-verbal cues, and voice pitch, hold a profound connection to happiness. The pursuit of meaningful relationships and the experience of genuine attraction can bring immense joy and fulfilment to our lives. When we find ourselves drawn to someone who aligns with our preferences, it can create a sense of excitement, connection, and emotional well-being. The reciprocation of attraction and the formation of deep, fulfilling bonds with a partner can contribute significantly to our overall happiness. Understanding the nuances of attraction allows us to navigate the complex landscape of relationships more effectively, fostering a greater likelihood of finding happiness in the realm of love and companionship.

Chapter XXI

Embracing the Wonders of Today and the Promises of Tomorrow

Our existence in this world is a complex tapestry of potentialities and inventions, each strand contributing to the weave of our future, a notion that resonates with Arthur C. Clarke's famous precept. This rule posits that when a seasoned yet elderly scientist declares something as impossible, they are likely mistaken. The true essence of this principle lies not so much in the inaccuracy of these predictions, but in their consistent inability to comprehend the dynamic nature of change.

Consider quantum mechanics and cosmology, for example. These scientific domains are incessantly expanding the limits of our knowledge, and in the process, they're moulding the future.

Let's explore quantum computing as a case in point. In the not-so-distant past, a computer leveraging the peculiar laws of quantum physics seemed as surreal as a tale spun in a science fiction novel. Quantum computers, with their capacity to process information at exponential rates far surpassing the capabilities of classical computers, were once a far-off dream. However, consider the narrative of a young researcher named Michelle Simmons. In Sydney, Australia, she and her team are building the world's first quantum computer in silicon, an achievement once deemed impossible. Major corporations like IBM and Google are also joining this technological race, turning the quantum computing dream into a palpable reality. This emerging technology promises to upend everything from pharmaceutical discovery to climate modelling, potentially improving our lives and contributing to worldwide happiness.

Space exploration, too, has experienced a transformation, with concepts once confined to science fiction becoming scientific endeavours. Consider the motivational story of Elon Musk and his enterprise, SpaceX. Musk's daring ambition to colonize Mars seemed like a wild fantasy when he first unveiled it. Nevertheless, today, SpaceX is conducting missions that are laying the groundwork for human voyages to Mars. The notion of humans stepping onto another planet, once a pure fantasy, is now within our collective reach, demonstrating how our quest for happiness may one day span beyond our home planet.

In the realm of medicine, we are witnessing the dawn of a new age with personalized treatments grounded in genomics. Imagine receiving a therapeutic regimen tailored specifically to your genetic makeup, enhancing treatment effectiveness and minimizing side effects. This is the current reality for individuals like Molly, a young woman who managed to find the right cancer treatment via genomic testing after numerous unsuccessful trials with conventional methods. What was once a distant star in the medical cosmos is now lighting the path towards a future where healthcare is personalized, enhancing patient satisfaction and overall happiness.

It's crucial to bear in mind that these ground-breaking developments are not mere extensions of our present; they signify transformative shifts in thinking, technology, and societal acceptance. The future, therefore, is not merely a reflection of the present, but a dynamic evolution, continuously moulded by innovation and the audacity to question the impossible.

Embracing the present involves recognizing the swift pace of change and the potential for transformation inherent in our current scientific endeavours. As we continue to push the boundaries of knowledge and possibility, we are effectively welcoming the future – a future not distant and abstract, but one being actively shaped by the currents of the present.

In this exploration of happiness, let's delve into the pivotal concept of embracing the here and now while welcoming the future with open arms.

Consider Quantum Computing. Once, it was a realm of fantasy, a notion too surreal to be true. But then enters Michelle Simmons, a daring quantum physicist, who embraced the improbable, pushing beyond the realms of the known. Today, she's at the helm of a team crafting the world's first silicon quantum computer. The lesson here? Be receptive to the new and unfamiliar, no matter how fantastical it may seem. This openness can lead to unforeseen avenues of opportunity and personal growth.

Then there's Elon Musk, a man with audacious dreams. Colonizing Mars was considered an impossibility, a laughable concept. However, Musk, with his "Dream Big, Start Small" philosophy, has been steadily turning science fiction into science fact, one small step at a time. The takeaway? Don't shy away from dreaming big, no matter how unreachable your goals seem. Break them down, act on them, and gradually, you'll inch closer to your dreams.

Consider the story of Molly. Through the power of genomic testing, Molly found the right cancer treatment, marking a triumph of personalized medicine. This breakthrough in patient care sends a potent message: there's no one-size-fits-all path to happiness. It's about tailoring your life experiences to your unique needs and aspirations, whether it's your diet, exercise routine, or learning style.

The future, as we know it, is not a mere projection of the present. It's an evolution, shaped by those audacious enough to challenge the status quo. Buckminster Fuller's words encapsulate this: "You never change things by fighting the existing reality. To change something, build a new model that makes the existing model obsolete." So, question the norm, explore uncharted territories, and don't be afraid to disrupt.

Embrace Change, a lesson that's more relevant than ever. Our world is undergoing an unprecedented rate of change. Although this can be overwhelming, adapting to change paves the way for personal growth and new possibilities. Remember, flexibility and lifelong learning are your allies in this ever-evolving world.

Lastly, the power of optimism cannot be overstated. The impossibilities of today could very well be the realities of tomorrow. Cultivate a mindset of positivity and trust in the potential of the future. This can foster resilience and engender greater happiness.

In essence, the quest for happiness isn't a destination but a continual journey. By keeping an open mind, daring to dream, personalizing your life, challenging the norm, embracing change, and fostering optimism, you can harness the wonders of today and the promises of tomorrow. You're not merely a spectator of the future but an active participant, shaping it in your pursuit of happiness.

Chapter XXII

The Predictive Power of Emotion in Decision-Making

In a world deeply entrenched in the ideologies of reasoning and logic, where we are persistently urged to 'think things through', the suggestion that our gut instincts can often serve as a trustworthy guide in decision-making may sound paradoxical. However, as we venture deeper into the intriguing expanse of human psychology, it becomes evident that the emotional forces shaping our intuition can often provide unique insights that strict, unyielding logic may fail to consider.

To demonstrate this concept, let's consider a fascinating study that examined the tug of war between logic and gut instinct in the decision-making process. The study involved participants being offered two distinct choices - a reproduction of an Impressionist painting and a poster of a humorous cartoon cat. While some participants were asked to employ logical reasoning to their choice, meticulously weighing the advantages and disadvantages, others were guided to follow their gut instinct, making a quick decision based on how each option made them feel.

What were the findings? Those who relied on their gut feelings, termed as 'pre feeling', were notably more content with their choice. They had successfully employed their emotions as a guiding force to navigate their decision. Conversely, the participants who relied on logical analysis ended up less satisfied with their selection.

This concept of 'pre feeling' highlights the incredible predictive capability of our emotions. Our current feelings can, astonishingly, serve as a gauge for our future satisfaction. However, like any intricate instrument, our emotional compass has its limitations. Our brain, always alert and tasked with perceiving reality, often struggles with the chore of envisioning one scenario while grappling with another. The neural resources that our brain uses to generate imaginary scenarios are the same ones it uses to process real-world experiences. This creates a form of competition where the pressing needs of the present often overpower our attempts to mentally simulate the future.

Therefore, while our gut feelings can provide valuable guidance, it's vital to bear in mind that our ability to predict future emotions can be obscured by the intensity of our current emotional state. This realization serves as a critical counterpoint, reminding us of the need for a balanced approach when utilizing our emotions as a guide.

As we navigate through this exploration, one thing becomes apparent: our emotions, often perceived as secondary considerations, hold a central role in our decision-making processes. They are not just fleeting states of being but are potent predictors of our future satisfaction. So, when you're next faced with a decision, you might want to pause, consult your gut, and question: what is my intuition telling me?

Our gut, our intuition, often detects subtle cues and patterns that our conscious mind may overlook. By checking in with our gut feelings, we can often gain additional insight into the choices we face.

While it's crucial to consider the logical aspects of a decision, don't disregard the wisdom of your intuition. Learn to trust your gut, and you'll be well on your way to making decisions that are more aligned with your true feelings and ultimate satisfaction.

The term 'pre feeling' is used describe the fascinating interplay between emotion and decision-making. This intriguing concept suggests that our gut feelings, our instinctual emotional responses, can be powerful predictors of future satisfaction. Like an internal compass, they often guide us towards what brings us joy. However, this compass doesn't always point north. Our emotional state in the present moment can sway our compass needle, leading us to misjudge how future scenarios might make us feel.

So, how can we use this newfound knowledge? How can we harness the power of pre feeling without falling into its potential pitfalls? Here are some strategies that might be beneficial:

Embrace the Emotional Check-In: Next time you find yourself at a crossroads, pause for a moment. Tune into your emotions. Ask yourself, "What is my intuition telling me?"

Respect the Emotional Context: We must recognize that our current emotional state can influence our perception of the future. If you're feeling particularly strong emotions, acknowledge them before making a decision. Your emotional context might be attempting to skew your compass needle off course.

The Balancing Act: Despite the power of our gut, we should not discard logic. There's a delicate balance between rational thinking and emotional intuition. Striving to maintain this balance is key. Your gut can guide you, but it shouldn't always have the final say.

The Art of Practice: Start with small, inconsequential decisions to get the hang of trusting your gut. As with any skill, proficiency comes with practice. Over time, you'll become more adept at understanding when your intuition is worth following.

As we explore the world of pre feeling, we begin to recognize the intricate interaction between our emotions and the decisions we make. Acknowledging this dynamic allows us to make choices that satisfy both our logical and emotional needs. So, the next time you're faced with a decision, don't forget to trust your gut. You might be surprised at where it leads you.

Part VIII

Perception, Time, and the Tapestry of Meaning

Chapter XXIII

An Exploration of Happiness, Repetition, and Human Perception

Buried beneath the complex fabric of human nature lies a peculiar paradox: the joy that once blossomed in our hearts seems to diminish with repeated exposure to the same experiences. This strange phenomenon, supported by a wealth of scientific evidence, narrates a captivating tale when viewed through the prism of everyday life.

In the carousel of childhood memories. The initial ride is a thrill, a roller-coaster of pure exhilaration. However, each subsequent whirl of the carousel dulls the thrill, reflecting the psychological principle of hedonic adaptation. This is the essence of the 'hedonic treadmill' concept, which posits that our happiness levels, after experiencing highs and lows, tend to revert back to a baseline.

So how do we escape this treadmill? It appears that variety and time manipulation are our best bet. The fascinating case of Joshua Bell, a renowned violinist, underscores the power of variety. Usually performing in packed concert halls, Bell once played incognito in a Washington D.C. metro station. The change in environment transformed the mundane into the magical, sparking joy and interest among the few who recognized the beauty in his music amidst the city's chaos.

But time, it seems, is the more potent tool for long-lasting happiness. Consider an upcoming vacation. The joy doesn't just spring from the trip itself, but also the moments we spend planning it. Sheldon and Lyubomirsky's 2010 study supports this, showing that manipulating the timing of pleasurable events can help us circumvent hedonic adaptation, thereby extending our happiness.

Interestingly, our penchant for variety often tricks us into conflating sequential options with simultaneous ones. It's akin to a child in a candy shop, believing that more candy equals more happiness. This fascinating misinterpretation offers a glimpse into our complex dance with time.

Time perception has always been a fascinating subject in psychology and neuroscience. A ground-breaking study published in "Science" in 2012 revealed that the more attention we give an event, the longer it seems to last. Waiting for a loved one at the airport is a prime example of this. As those final moments before their arrival stretch out, we are reminded of how our perception of time affects our happiness.

Despite the popular belief that variety is the spice of life, it may be our mastery over time that is the real game-changer in our pursuit of happiness. Consider the practice of mindful meditation, where the focus is on savouring the present moment. By concentrating on the 'now', practitioners often report experiencing a deep sense of happiness and peace.

Ultimately, in the vast landscape of life, it's not merely the passage of time, but our perception and manipulation of it that shapes our happiness. This insight leads us to a radical rethinking of happiness. The secret to enduring joy may lie not so much in the diversity of our experiences, but rather in our mastery over time perception. This fascinating paradox, a central aspect of our human nature, is a product of the ebbing joy from repeated experiences. A wealth of scientific studies supports this, showing how we often counteract this through variety and time, with time playing a more crucial role in the long run.

This tendency sheds light on our inclination to mistake sequential options for simultaneous ones, offering compelling insight into our understanding of time and its profound impact on our happiness. Grounded in empirical research, it's clear that our joy tends to fade with repetition, a concept that aligns with the principle of hedonic adaptation.

In our battle against this hedonic adaptation, we naturally lean towards two primary strategies: variety and time. Variety introduces new elements into our experiences, providing a temporary boost to our joy. However, time proves to be more effective in the long run. This is supported by a 2010 study by Sheldon and Lyubomirsky, which reveals that judiciously altering the timing of pleasurable experiences can deter the process of hedonic adaptation, thereby extending our happiness.

In the grand scheme of life, it's not just the passage of time but our perception and manipulation of it that shapes our happiness. This insight prompts a radical reconsideration of our approach to happiness. The key to lasting joy may not reside so much in the variety of our experiences but rather in our ability to master time perception.

Chapter XXIV

Unravelling Time's Perceptive Intricacies

Navigating the labyrinth of human time perception and its resulting impact on our predictions of the future is akin to unearthing the intricacies of our cognitive peculiarities. The brain, though a marvel of nature, is prone to misconceptions and fallacies in the realm of time perception and prognostications of future events. Our imaginations, unshackled by the constraints of reality, weave intricate narratives that often misguide us in our temporal estimates, culminating in unanticipated errors in our judgments.

The human brain's unique capacity to perceive time and forecast the future has been a topic of fervent interest among researchers. Time perception is a personal experience that can vary widely between individuals and even within the same individual under different conditions. For instance, the age-old adage of a watched pot never boiling, or the rapid passage of time during an engaging activity, illustrates the ease with which our perception of time can be distorted and our future event predictions can be significantly astray.

Our imagination, one of the leading causes of these errors, conjures images devoid of temporal markers, resulting in a warped perception of time. A research conducted by Wittmann and Paulus in 2008 provided empirical evidence of this phenomenon. The study found that a time interval filled with varied and intense experiences is perceived as longer than an equivalent period dominated by monotony. This proves that our imaginations often exaggerate the intensity and variety of future experiences, leading us to misestimate the time they will occupy.

The concept of anchoring, the reliance on initial pieces of information to make subsequent judgments, is another critical facet of time perception. As demonstrated by a study by Jacowitz and Kahneman in 1995, our minds lean on the first piece of information we encounter as a reference point, significantly influencing our time estimations and future forecasts. Thus, our current state or emotions can skew our future predictions, leading to potential miscalculations.

It's also important to underline the role of emotions in our perception of time. Our current emotional state can tint our expectations and distort our perception of future events. Numerous studies, such as one by Droit-Volet, Brunot, and Niedenthal in 2004, have shown that participants in a happy state perceived time as passing faster than those in a sad state. Therefore, our current emotional state has the potential to mislead our future selves, leading to misconceptions about time's passage.

Further, our cultural and societal contexts also shape our perception of time. The way different cultures perceive and value time influences how individuals within these cultures predict future events. A study by Levine in 1997 showed that people from cultures that prioritize punctuality and scheduling tend to be more accurate in their time estimates than those from cultures with a more fluid concept of time.

The exploration of time perception and its intricacies is indeed a journey into the mind's labyrinth. Despite our cognitive prowess, our brains are susceptible to certain biases and distortions in time perception and future predictions. Factors such as our imagination, anchoring effects, emotions, and cultural contexts all contribute to shaping our perceptions and leading us astray in our future predictions.

Studying time perception offers an intriguing insight into the human mind's workings, illuminating how our current feelings and experiences can mislead our future selves. By comprehending these distortions and fallacies, we can strive to improve our future predictions, thereby enhancing our decision-making and planning capacities. Delving into the complexity of time perception, although challenging, promises to yield substantial insights in our quest to understand ourselves and the world we inhabit. As we continue to untangle these mysteries, we realize that the journey itself, much like time perception, is subjective and replete with surprises.

Chapter XXV

How History Influences Our Perception of Value

The human brain, an intricate labyrinth of thoughts, emotions, and recollections, exhibits an intriguing tendency to reminisce. This lingering fondness for the past sends waves through our reasoning, resulting in varied assessments of identical situations. Intriguingly, our perception of value and gratification isn't based solely on definitive metrics. Instead, it's a vibrant mosaic shaped by comparisons to and contrasts with our history, profoundly influencing the choices we make. When debating the expense of your daily brew or contemplating a substantial investment, it's crucial to understand it's not solely about the end figures. The journey is a psychological exploration into the captivating universe of relative measures and the eccentricities of human perception steering our decisions.

To better appreciate this captivating sphere, let's guide our discussion through the lens of scientific investigation. Take a mental trip back to the 1980s when Kahneman and Tversky first acquainted us with the concept of "loss aversion." According to their research, subjects were more inclined to steer clear of losses than to seek equivalent gains. This propensity to avert losses is frequently intensified by our connection to historical values, leading us to overvalue what we risk losing versus what we stand to gain.

Let's traverse to a familiar setting - a cosy coffee shop. Just a year ago, your regular cup of coffee was priced at $1, but today, it costs twice as much. Your evaluation of the coffee's worth isn't solely dependent on the updated price, but it's also relative to the increase from the past. Even if the coffee still delights your palate as it once did, your perception of its worth is influenced by the increased expense. This seemingly trivial example illustrates how our associations with past experiences, as mundane as a coffee's cost, can affect our current assessments.

Expanding the scope, consider purchasing a vehicle. You may stumble upon a fantastic bargain, priced significantly below market value. However, if you recall that same vehicle advertised for a lower price a month ago, your excitement over the deal might dwindle. The car's intrinsic value remains unchanged, yet your perception of its worth has been adjusted by a past price, influencing your purchasing decision.

In our data-rich era, our minds often employ heuristics, or cognitive shortcuts, to facilitate decision-making. These expedients, while handy for accelerating our decision-making process, can occasionally mislead us. Simonson and Tversky (1992) proposed the notion of "context-dependent preferences", where the availability or absence of an alternative could reverse our preference. For instance, given a choice between a $100 cash voucher and a high-quality pen valued at $120, you might opt for the cash. However, introduce a third option - a less expensive pen worth $50 - and you may find yourself preferring the more expensive pen. The value of the initial two options remains stable, but your preference alters, influenced by the memory of the cheaper pen.

These instances underscore how our perception of value and gratification is shaped not only by the present but also by historical experiences and comparisons. As we navigate life, making innumerable decisions daily, it's important to remain aware of these cognitive biases that might subtly manipulate our choices.

So, whether you're contemplating the price of your daily cup of coffee or deliberating a significant investment, remember the fascinating dynamics of relative measures and the idiosyncrasies of human perception. In a world that frequently encourages objectivity, acknowledging and understanding the subjective shades of our decision-making can facilitate more satisfying and informed choices.

Part IX

Navigating Change, Wellness, and Collective Consciousness

Chapter XXVI

The Enigmatic Paradox of New Beginnings

Does the thrill of new acquisitions quickly dissipate for you? Or have you noticed how our perception of gains and losses shifts depending on comparative factors? These intriguing facets of human psychology are what this investigation seeks to decipher through the prism of scientific research. As we journey into the intricate workings of the mind, expect to be prompted to reassess your own assumptions, gain deep comprehension of our cognitive operations, and understand the extensive role that comparison plays in shaping our emotions.

Inherently, humans are attracted to the allure of the new. There's a certain exhilaration attached to it, isn't there? The smell of a freshly printed book, the thrill of driving a car straight from the showroom, or the excitement of exploring a new locale — these instances have an initial mesmerizing impact on our senses. However, with the passage of time, this fascination seems to dull, and what was once an enchanting novelty eventually becomes ordinary, even outdated. We need to ponder over the question — why is that so?

To shed light on this conundrum, we consider a study conducted by Dr. Roberta Schriber of the University of New York. Her research revolves around the notion of 'hedonic adaptation,' an idea that encapsulates how we, as humans, swiftly adjust to fresh circumstances or things, leading to a gradual decrease in our emotional reactions over time. For example, a newly acquired smartphone becomes just another item once we familiarize ourselves with it. This innate tendency to adapt, though crucial for our survival, often diminishes our appreciation for novelty.

But what if the plot of our diminishing enthusiasm extends further? Let's explore another psychological aspect: the effect of comparisons on our interpretation of gains and losses. When we acquire something new, the initial elation is often fuelled by a comparison with our previous possessions. However, as time passes, newer, more appealing options come into our purview, and all of a sudden, our once-cherished possession appears less valuable.

In this context, let's consider the research conducted by Professor Daniel Gilbert of Harvard University. His investigations on 'affective forecasting' suggest that humans are notoriously poor at predicting their future emotional states. We consistently downplay the impact of comparisons on our emotions, resulting in disappointment or dissatisfaction when our expectations fail to match reality.

This element of comparison extends beyond our material possessions. It permeates our self-perception, values, and life experiences. We frequently evaluate our achievements, not in absolute terms, but in relation to those around us. This behaviour is understood through Leon Festinger's 'social comparison theory.' According to this theory, we inherently compare ourselves with others to evaluate our abilities and beliefs. While this can be instrumental for self-improvement, it can also lead to a decrease in self-worth and heightened dissatisfaction if not handled with care.

As we delve deeper into the human mind, it becomes evident that the fluid nature of comparisons significantly shapes our experiences. Ignoring this dynamic element often results in the underestimation of future experiences.

An interesting case study that highlights this point is the research conducted by Nobel laureate Daniel Kahneman on 'Prospect Theory.' According to his theory, people usually place higher value on a potential loss than on a similar gain. This explains why losing $100 might induce more disappointment than the happiness one would derive from finding the same amount. The shifting comparisons underlying this behaviour underline the complex workings of human cognition.

Approaching the conclusion of this exploration, one may question — how can we leverage these insights to enhance our lives? The answer lies in developing a deeper awareness of the psychological mechanisms influencing our behaviour. By recognizing the fleeting nature of novelty, we can foster a more enduring form of joy. By understanding the impact of comparisons, we can aim to appreciate our possessions and achievements on their own merits, rather than in relative terms.

Adopting these insights could enhance our ability to accurately predict future emotions and sidestep the pitfalls of unrealistic expectations. Our initial fascination with novelty, while enticing, can lead us to overestimate the longevity of our future happiness. By acknowledging the reality of hedonic adaptation, we can recalibrate our expectations and learn to derive pleasure from the familiar as much as from the novel.

Moreover, by acknowledging the role of comparisons in determining our perception of value, we can make more informed decisions that align with our enduring happiness, rather than ephemeral moments of joy. For instance, understanding that our satisfaction with a new purchase might decrease once we begin comparing it with newer models can guide us towards more considered decisions about what we truly need and value.

Furthermore, accepting the social comparison theory doesn't mean we succumb to unhealthy comparisons. Instead, we can utilize it as a tool for self-improvement and self-understanding. By acknowledging our instinctive inclination to measure our abilities and beliefs against others, we can opt to compare ourselves to people who inspire growth, rather than those who induce feelings of inadequacy.

Lastly, by recognizing the implications of Prospect Theory, we can gain better insight into our decision-making patterns, especially under uncertain conditions. This understanding can help us curb the impact of loss aversion and make decisions that truly reflect our preferences, rather than being swayed by the fear of potential losses.

The intricate human mind, with its complex mechanisms and profound depths, offers us valuable insights into our behaviour, preferences, and emotions. Exploring these intriguing psychological phenomena not only equips us with a deeper understanding of ourselves but also empowers us to lead more fulfilling and joyous lives. This exploration stands as a testament to the limitless marvels of human psychology, constantly reminding us that the more we learn about our minds, the more there is to discover.

Chapter XXVII

Unveiling Invisible Tracks to Joy and Wellness

Prepare yourself for an unconventional journey into the realms of wellness and fulfilment, one that challenges standard paradigms of health and happiness. Forget seeking solace in the tranquil refuge of your yoga mat, the promises encased within vitamin capsules, or the artistry of a cosmetic surgeon's scalpel.

Instead, welcome to a universe shaped by extraordinary narratives of those who have journeyed through the furnace of adversity and not only survived but were reborn. We will delve into the stories of politicians who have withstood the typhoon of public humiliation, former convicts who have tasted the sourness of unwarranted confinement, and celebrities whose glamorous existence was abruptly overshadowed by paralysis. These individuals serve as testimonials that their tribulations catapulted them to satisfaction peaks once considered unattainable.

You might question, "How can public humiliation, unwarranted imprisonment, or sudden paralysis possibly augment well-being?" A reasonable query, indeed, as it rattles our existing ideologies. However, let's dissect what the latest scientific investigations propose.

Remarkably, we, as humans, inherently possess the ability to bounce back from trauma. The resilience of the human spirit, its capacity to adjust, endure, and thrive following adversity, has been meticulously explored within the domain of positive psychology. This chapter will investigate the fascinating concept of post-traumatic growth, a phenomenon where individuals report enhanced personal strength, a redefined perspective on life, and enriched relationships post traumatic events.

In our quest to decipher the often paradoxical relationship between adversity and happiness, numerous research initiatives offer valuable insights. Collectively, they shed light on the extraordinary human capacity to adapt, endure, and even prosper amidst life's tribulations.

One such ground-breaking study is led by psychologist Daniel Gilbert, the author of "Stumbling on Happiness". Gilbert and his team scrutinized the concept of "affective forecasting", our ability to predict our emotional future. Their results revealed that people generally exaggerate the negative consequences of adverse events. This is primarily due to our "psychological immune system", a term introduced by Gilbert, which signifies our inherent ability to adapt and discover happiness even in hardship.

In one of Gilbert's investigations, the happiness indices of lottery winners and paraplegics were compared a year following their life-altering event. Intriguingly, there was no significant difference in the overall contentment between the two groups. This outcome underscores our inherent ability to adapt to new circumstances—both prosperous and calamitous—quicker than we foresee.

Another significant research project is the series of studies on post-traumatic growth conducted by psychologists Richard Tedeschi and Lawrence Calhoun. They concluded that such adversities could lead to increased appreciation of life, enhanced personal strength, improved relationships, and the revelation of previously unrecognized paths and possibilities.

One of their studies engaged survivors of various traumatic events, including severe illness, accidents, and the loss of loved ones. The researchers found that a considerable fraction of participants reported experiencing transformation and growth following their ordeal.

Another study worth noting is the research on resilience by George Bonanno, a clinical psychologist at Columbia University. Bonanno's research suggests that resilience is actually the typical response to loss or trauma, debunking the common belief that such experiences usually lead individuals into extended periods of depression. Numerous individuals recover to their prior mental health and productivity levels relatively swiftly, affirming our inherent capacity to recuperate from adversity.

Combined, these studies weave an intriguing narrative: while adversity and negative events can undeniably inflict pain, they often impact our long-term happiness less than we might predict. They can even serve as catalysts for growth, resilience, and newfound fulfilment, allowing us to discover strengths and potentials we might never have unearthed otherwise.

Mindfulness, a concept originating from ancient Eastern philosophies, primarily Buddhism, has gained acknowledgment in contemporary psychology for its profound benefits. It represents a state of profound awareness of the present moment, free of judgment or resistance, and includes an assortment of practices designed to nurture this attentiveness.

As humans, we have a natural tendency to ruminate over past mistakes or anticipate future issues, especially when faced with challenging situations. This can initiate a stress and anxiety cycle that magnifies the original problem. However, mindfulness breaks this cycle by refocusing our attention to the present moment.

Numerous studies have illustrated the effectiveness of mindfulness in nurturing resilience in the face of adversity. For instance, a study published in "The Lancet" in 2015 found that mindfulness-based cognitive therapy (MBCT) was as effective as medication in preventing relapses in individuals with recurrent depression. The practice assisted participants in breaking free from patterns of negative thinking, enabling them to react to challenging situations with increased clarity and tranquillity.

Another study conducted at the University of Utah discovered that individuals with higher mindfulness scores were better at regulating their emotional responses. They reported lower levels of emotional instability, moodiness, and anxiety under stressful conditions.

Mindfulness can also aid us in accepting our circumstances. Acceptance is not about surrendering or admitting defeat, but about recognizing the reality of the situation without resistance. This acceptance can relieve us from the additional burden of emotional struggle, enabling us to perceive our situation more clearly and react more effectively.

In essence, mindfulness practices provide a potent path to navigate adversity. By fostering a non-judgmental awareness of the present moment, they enable us to respond to challenges with greater serenity, clarity, and compassion, paving the way for resilience, growth, and ultimately, improved well-being.

Let's consider strategies to promote a growth mindset. This concept, pioneered by psychologist Carol S. Dweck, suggests that our skills and intelligence can be cultivated through commitment and hard work. When adversity arises, those with a growth mindset perceive it not as a cul-de-sac but as an opportunity for learning and growth. Techniques to foster a growth mindset include embracing challenges, persisting in the face of setbacks, and understanding that effort is a path to mastery.

In contrast to the fixed mindset, which proposes that our abilities and intelligence are largely unchangeable, the growth mindset asserts that these qualities can be nurtured and expanded through dedication, persistence, and appropriate strategies.

When adversity looms, a growth mindset allows individuals to perceive it not as an insurmountable obstacle but as a stepping-stone towards personal development and success. Here are some practical strategies to foster a growth mindset:

Embrace Challenges: Treat each challenge as an opportunity to learn and advance. Instead of evading difficulties, confront them. Remember, it's in the process of tackling tough tasks that you stretch your abilities and make new progress.

Persist Despite Setbacks: Persistence in the face of setbacks is a key trait of a growth mindset. Understand that failure is not a reflection of your ability, but rather a part of the learning process. Reflect on what went wrong and strategize about how to approach the problem differently next time.

Cherish Effort: Recognize that effort isn't simply about toiling harder but also about labouring more intelligently. Applaud the journey of learning, not just the ultimate outcome. Make a routine of scrutinizing your performance and seeking ways to enhance.

Cultivate a Love for Learning: Revel in the process of learning for its own merit, rather than fixating solely on performance outcomes. This can help maintain your enthusiasm and motivation, even when progress appears slow or the work becomes challenging.

Welcome Feedback: Constructive feedback is crucial for growth. Rather than retreating from criticism, perceive it as valuable information that can facilitate your improvement.

Practice Flexible Thinking: Learn to perceive problems from varied perspectives. This can help you discover fresh solutions and strategies to surmount obstacles.

Nurture a Sense of Purpose: Having a sense of purpose can fuel motivation and persistence. This involves setting meaningful goals and envisaging how your personal growth contributes to these objectives.

By integrating these strategies into your daily life, you can cultivate a growth mindset that transforms adversity into a pathway for growth, mastery, and success. This shift in mindset can be empowering, leading to heightened resilience, improved performance, and a greater sense of fulfilment in all life's areas.

Chapter XXVIII

Harnessing Collective Wisdom in an Interconnected World

As we confront the uncertainty of tomorrow, our path forward is shrouded in mystery. The future may be enigmatic, but we are nonetheless compelled to make pivotal choices that will chart our direction. So, how can we effectively navigate this ambiguous territory? The solution is as ancient as mankind itself: communication and learning from one another.

Since the dawn of human existence, we have battled ignorance with the powerful weapon of shared knowledge. From early human cave drawings that passed on successful hunting techniques to future generations, to contemporary scientific research papers that expand our comprehension of the cosmos, we have always depended significantly on vicarious knowledge. Though this knowledge comes to us filtered and interpreted, we confer upon it a considerable degree of trust, letting it shape our world-view.

In today's digital epoch, we are interconnected more than ever before. A simple screen tap offers us entry to the communal wisdom of billions. This enormous knowledge network encompasses educators, friends, relatives, and even unknown individuals from around the world. Given this vast pool of knowledge, one might predict an extraordinary evolution in human decision-making. However, paradoxically, despite this unprecedented access to human experience, many persist in making less than optimal choices.

Consider, for example, the pervasive hesitancy towards vaccination, despite overwhelming scientific evidence of their advantages. The World Health Organization listed vaccine hesitancy among the top ten global health threats in 2019. Despite the availability of clear, accessible information, many individuals yield to misinformation, illustrating the crucial role of discernment in our reliance on vicarious knowledge.

Are we, then, overly trusting in others' words, or are we simply not trusting enough? The response isn't as straightforward as one might expect; it's a complex interplay between the two. The essence of decision-making lies in striking the delicate equilibrium between trusting others and exercising our independent judgment. This isn't an invitation to scepticism or cynicism, but rather a call to critical thinking and discernment.

Numerous instances from scientific research underscore the significance of discernment. The replication crisis in psychology, where many high-profile studies failed to replicate, underscores the necessity of scepticism and verification. The debate surrounding climate change offers another example, highlighting the perils of misinformation and the importance of placing faith in scientific consensus over baseless opinions.

Assessing the credibility of information sources and refining critical thinking abilities are crucial tools for navigating today's interconnected world. We present practical guidance on these aspects, enriched with scientific research and real-life illustrations.

Author Credentials: Begin by scrutinizing the author's qualifications and professional history. In scientific research, credibility is often conferred upon authors with relevant academic backgrounds or affiliations with recognized institutions.

Verification through Multiple Sources: Comparing information across diverse sources helps ascertain its credibility. If a piece of information is backed by multiple credible sources, it is likely accurate.

Recency: Particularly in fields such as science and technology, information evolves rapidly. Ensure the information source is current and up-to-date.

Peer Review: In academia, peer-reviewed articles are a trusted information source because they undergo rigorous evaluation by field experts.

Bias and Objectivity: Be alert to potential biases in both the source and your perception. Trustworthy sources present facts objectively, devoid of emotional language or baseless opinions.

Question Assumptions: Avoid accepting information at face value. Pose probing queries to understand the basis of claims. The scientific method teaches us to formulate and test hypotheses, a technique adaptable to everyday life.

Logical Reasoning: Cultivate logical reasoning skills to comprehend cause-and-effect relationships. Understanding the scientific workings behind vaccines and their interaction with the immune system, for instance, can lead to more informed decisions.

Open-mindedness: Maintain an open mind and be prepared to revise your stance when confronted with new information, echoing the scientific principle of falsifiability.

Reflective Thinking: Routinely evaluate your beliefs and opinions. This introspection facilitates personal growth and fosters understanding of how your biases and experiences might sway your judgment.

Balancing trust in others with personal judgment requires considering the source of advice and your own knowledge and instincts about the subject matter. Trusting a climate scientist's viewpoint on global warming, given their field expertise, is reasonable. But, if a claim, such as a product promising overnight weight loss, appears too good to be true, your personal judgment should prompt questioning the claim's validity.

Furthermore, research emphasizes the value of diversity in decision-making. A University of Michigan study revealed that diverse groups made more precise decisions than homogenous groups, attributable to a range of perspectives. This shows that while seeking others' opinions, it is beneficial to solicit diverse viewpoints.

In conclusion, nurturing the ability to discern reliable information and fostering critical thinking is an ongoing journey. The act of balancing trust in others with personal judgment is nuanced and context-dependent. By honing these skills, we can enhance our decision-making capabilities, better equipping us to tackle the uncertainties of the future.

Conclusion

In the course of this book, we have embarked on a journey that challenges conventional wisdom and invites us to explore the hidden paths to joy, wellness, and fulfillment. We have delved into the realms of adversity, resilience, mindfulness, and decision-making, uncovering profound insights and practical strategies that can transform our lives.

The paradoxical relationship between adversity and happiness has been a central theme throughout our exploration. We have witnessed the incredible resilience of the human spirit, as individuals not only survive but thrive in the face of adversity. The concept of post-traumatic growth has shown us that traumatic events can lead to personal strength, a redefined perspective on life, and enriched relationships. Adversity, it turns out, can be a catalyst for growth and newfound fulfillment.

Mindfulness, rooted in ancient wisdom, has emerged as a powerful tool in navigating life's challenges. By cultivating a non-judgmental awareness of the present moment, mindfulness allows us to break free from the cycle of stress and anxiety, enabling us to respond to difficulties with serenity, clarity, and compassion. It teaches us to accept our circumstances without resistance, empowering us to find new paths and possibilities even in the midst of adversity.

The growth mindset, championed by Carol Dweck, has provided us with a transformative perspective on setbacks and challenges. Instead of seeing them as insurmountable obstacles, we can view them as opportunities for learning and personal development. By embracing challenges, persisting in the face of setbacks, and valuing effort and learning, we can cultivate a mindset that propels us forward, enabling us to reach new levels of resilience, mastery, and fulfillment.

As we navigate the interconnected world of today, the importance of discernment and critical thinking cannot be overstated. We have learned the significance of assessing the credibility of information sources, verifying claims through multiple sources, and questioning assumptions. Balancing trust in others with personal judgment, while embracing diverse perspectives, allows us to make informed decisions and navigate the complexities of our interconnected world.

In conclusion, this book has offered us a fresh perspective on well-being and fulfillment, unveiling the invisible tracks that lead us to joy and wellness. It has shown us that adversity, though challenging, can be a springboard for growth and resilience. It has introduced us to the transformative power of mindfulness, enabling us to find peace and clarity amidst life's storms. It has inspired us to cultivate a growth mindset, turning setbacks into stepping-stones for personal development. And it has emphasized the importance of discernment and critical thinking in an interconnected world.

As we close this chapter of our journey, let us carry these insights with us, armed with the knowledge and tools to navigate life's ups and downs with grace, resilience, and an open mind. May we continue to embrace the unexpected and unseen pathways that often lead to our most profound moments of bliss and fulfillment. By harnessing collective wisdom, cultivating resilience, and fostering mindful awareness, we can create a life filled with joy, wellness, and a deep sense of fulfillment.

While every precaution has been taken in the preparation of this book, the publisher assumes no responsibility for errors or omissions, or for damages resulting from the use of the information contained herein.

THE HAPPINESS BLUEPRINT

First edition. February 21, 2024.

Copyright © 2024 Ana Pachuashvili.

Written by Ana Pachuashvili.